Growing Vegetables

*DIY Guide to Master Vegetable
Cultivation at Home Starting From Zero
How to Grow Healthy Food and Make Profit*

Thiago P.K. Land

Table of Contents

Pruning Shears
Kneeling Pad
Tool Storage

Selling Produce
Selling Seeds
Selling Plants
Run a U-Pick Garden
Begin a CSA or Subscription Service

Part 2: Building Your Garden

What Makes a Good Garden Space?

How much sun is in your area?
How saturated is your soil?
How close is the garden to your source of water?
How busy is the area you are gardening in?
Is there some sort of structure that will impact growth in your location?
Matching Plants to the Right Places

Choosing Garden Beds or Ground for Gardening

Garden beds
Growing in the soil

Build Your Garden

Bush Tomatoes
Cabbage
Carrots
Celery
Chard
Garlic
Green Beans (String Beans, Bush Beans, Pole Beans)
Kale
Head Lettuce
Onions (Leeks, Scallions, etc.)
Parsnips
Peas
Potatoes
Radishes
Spinach
Turnips
Watermelon

Chapter 9: Planting Full Sunlight Vegetables ... 107

Acorn Squash (Winter Squashes)
Beans (Pod/Runner Beans)
Cauliflower
Corn
Cucumbers
Eggplant
Okra
Peppers
Pumpkins
Sweet Potatoes
Tomatillos
Vine Tomatoes
Zucchini (Summer Squashes)

Part 4: Maintaining and Troubleshooting Your Garden

Part 5: Monetizing Your Garden

Introduction

If you've got land to spare, you've probably wondered how you could start making use of it. Gardening allows you to start growing food that you can enjoy at home. You can grow fruits and veggies that don't have to go through processing or shipping. That means that they not only taste better, but they also have more nutrients. Did you know that food rapidly loses nutrients after being harvested? Foods like lettuce can lose 30% of their nutrients just three days after harvesting them. And, the produce that you buy at the store is significantly older than three days old. By the time most produce gets to your table, it's traveled 1500 miles. However, these days, people are more and more eager for new options that will allow them to get their food much sooner. You could, for example, grow your own produce. This is a fantastic option if you have space. You can also purchase veggies that were locally grown at your local farmer's markets.

In recent years, there has been a shift toward putting local food on the table, and much of that is purchased at farmer's markets. When you get food at a farmer's market, it has been picked at the peak of perfection and then delivered locally, cutting down the distance that the food has to travel, and consequently, also cutting down the time it takes to get to your table.

Now, some people who start gardening for themselves also realize that they have plenty of extra produce. Why not take that produce and start passing it on? By growing extras, you don't have to do much more work than you would if you were raising your veggies at home just for yourself, but you get the added bonus of getting to sell it off.

Or, you could even design an entire business model around gardening and grow enough to profit from the surplus regularly. You have a myriad of options for ensuring that you get that extra cash in your pocket while you garden. If you are determined, you can start growing vegetables, and those veggies will make money for you. You just have to get started.

When you read this book, you dig into vegetable gardening. This is a beginner's guide to growing-it-yourself veggies. When you grow your own vegetables, you start on a path that is rewarding, affordable, and delicious. Whether you're new to gardening or interested in saving costs, this book will offer you easy-to-follow steps that you can use to start, grow, and sustain your own garden.

Learning the basics of starting your dream garden will prepare you for everything you'll need to go from newbie to pro gardener in just a few simple chapters. Through reading this book, you will get the basics of growing your own plants at home, starting your garden, planning it out, and more. You'll be guided through cultivating different veggies that can be grown in a variety of environments, including both sun- and shade-loving plants. You'll discover how to care for your garden from planning through harvest and beyond.

Now, if you're ready to go from greenhorn to green thumb, keep reading. From being able to garden to selling the fruits—or veggies, in this case—of your labor, you will discover everything that you need.

Part 1:

Understanding Gardening

Chapter 1:
Everything Your Plants
Need to Thrive

Plants are simple things. They are autotrophic by nature, meaning that they generate their own fuel to be able to survive. They can take sunlight to create the energy they need in a process known as photosynthesis. As your plants take in sunlight, they harness the power of light and use it to process carbon dioxide and water to produce sugar (glucose). It's this glucose that powers the plant through its biological processes.

All plants require just a few things for them to survive. If you want your plants to thrive, you just make sure to provide them with the basics. They will need water, carbon dioxide, and sunlight, and nutrients. That's right—soil is not actually a necessity for growing plants. While that is where they tend to grow naturally, there are ways that you can grow your plants without it. Plants can be grown without soil in a process known as hydroponic gardening. This method provides water, air and nutrient circulation, and light to promote growth. This book is working on the premise that you will be gardening in soil, but there is an amazing amount of literature available to you if hydroponics is something that interests you. To learn more about traditional gardening, keep reading!

Now, let's go over the basics of what you'll need for your plants to thrive.

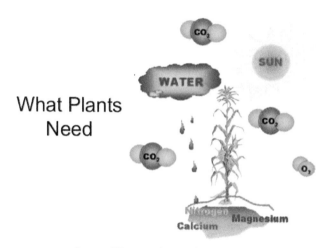

What Plants Need

- your garden will require a few simple elements to grow properly-

Water

Water is one of the essentials. When you don't have water, your plant cannot live. This is simply since your plants will not have that necessary component of photosynthesis. Without the water, the plant cannot create the sugars it needs to use for energy.

Just like your body needs sugar to function, you need to allow your plant the ability to build that sugar as well.

Your plant needs a certain amount of water, but too much water can also create problems. You have to give your plants just the right amount of water so they can generate sugar, but not so much water that they drown. Too much water can actually kill your plants because your plants' roots are responsible for gas exchange. If the roots are covered in water, they can't transfer gases. The result is that the roots can drown and begin to rot. If that occurs, the plant dies.

Watering your plants the right way will be dependent upon the particular plant that you are growing. Vegetables require you to provide a lot of water to them because they tend to have those higher water contents, especially vegetables such as cucumbers or lettuce. We will be taking a closer look at watering and watering methods when we get to Chapter 11.

Carbon Dioxide

Carbon dioxide is one of the other necessities for your plant. Your plant requires carbon dioxide to perform photosynthesis. A simple equation explains this: You take six carbon dioxide molecules, six water molecules, and sunlight, and together, you create a single molecule of glucose (sugar). The rest is converted to oxygen. This means that your plant needs a way to bring that carbon dioxide in and then puts out oxygen, much in the way you breathe air.

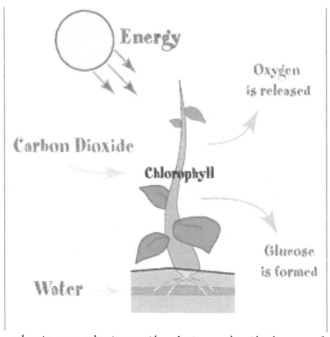

- plants use photosynthesis to make their own fuel in the form of simple sugars -

As we require oxygen, so do plants require carbon dioxide. Plants bring in CO2 through their roots, which is why having healthy, non-compacted soil is so vital. But plants also bring in carbon dioxide through their leaves, using the tiny pores (called stomata) that you can see on the underside of each leaf. These stomata take in carbon dioxide and release oxygen in a process known as respiration. Ensuring you plant your garden with enough space to allow proper airflow is another key to having thriving vegetables. If you've ever been in a crowded room and needed to step outside for some air, you'll understand why your garden needs room to breathe.

Sunlight

Sunlight is essential for plants to grow. Your plants use sunlight as that catalyst that creates the energy that plants need. When it comes to providing plants with sunlight, you can use several different methods. You can, for example, grow your plants outside, which is obviously the preferred method. You can also get grow lights, which provide artificial ultraviolet light and allow you to cultivate plants in an indoor environment. Many dedicated gardeners use both by starting delicate seeds inside before transplanting them into the garden soil.

The key to sunlight, however, is that your plants only need so much of it. Just leaving your plants in daylight or bright lights can be problematic. Your plants need time in the darkness, so following each plant's requirements is very important. Plants tend to be categorized in three different ways: Full light, partial shade, and full shade. All plants need to have their light needs met to their recommended requirements, or you will see abnormal growth.

Full sunlight plants require a minimum of 8 hours a day in direct light. This means that they have to actually be in the sunlight the entire time, not just outside in the shade of a tree. You want to make sure that the plants are there, soaking up the rays. Sun-loving plants are typically grown in the summer, where they can take advantage of the longer days. Partial sunlight plants usually require between 4 and 6 hours of light per day to grow to their proper specifications. Full shade plants need protection from direct sunlight altogether. The plants must avoid being directly shone upon because they can burn or scald.

Of course, there are other ways that light can be divided up as well, primarily in either direct or indirect classifications. These classifications are precisely what they sound like but don't often apply to the plants you'll be considering for a vegetable garden. It's just a nice thing to be aware of if you want to expand your gardening palate in the future and branch out into landscaping. We'll talk more about providing proper light for your vegetables when discussing how to site your garden properly.

Nutrients

Nutrients are the last essential component to having a thriving vegetable garden. Like animals, plants have different nutritional and dietary needs. They need to get that somehow, and usually, nutrients are gained through the roots. As plants absorb water from the soil, they also take up any nutrients that are present. The soil that plants grow in must be able to provide these nutrients, or your vegetables will have a failure to thrive. Soil naturally contains nutrients from the decomposition of plants, animals, and bedrock, but it can become depleted. If your soil is unhealthy, you need to work to replace those nutrients and organic material with fertilizers and compost, which we'll discuss in-depth later in the book.

Chapter 2:
Tools and Supplies
for Beginner Gardeners

When you have an understanding of what your plants will require, the next step is to learn about the tools you'll need to make your garden a reality. There is a myriad of tool options out there, and much of it is based on personal preference, but gardening is much more efficient when you have the right tools for the job. In this chapter, we're going to explore many of the basic tools you'll want to have at your disposal, giving you the ability to make informed choices.

Keep in mind that acquiring tools doesn't need to be expensive, and it's possible to find a ton of functional items on local buy/sell/trade boards, flea markets and fairs, and at discount retailers. Sometimes a little TLC is all it takes to bring a secondhand tool back to life, and sometimes it behooves you to spend a little money for a high-quality tool that will last a lifetime with proper maintenance. And sometimes, it's just nice to treat yourself to a new gardening gadget. It's all up to your tastes and budget. Let's go over the tool list now, and you can make a shopping list that fits your needs.

- the right tools will make your gardening efforts that much easier -

Shovels

Shovels are one of the most important tools that you will need. Having a shovel will allow you to move large amounts of soil from place to place as necessary. For example, you might need to dig up a hole to install large new plants, like fruit trees. At a bare minimum, you'll need to use an angled shovel in your gardening. You want to be able to dig holes, move soil, or even relocate plants. Now, you might think that shovels are shovels. But you should choose one that is comfortable for you. You want to find a handle that is thick enough to be comfortable for you, as well as being a suitable material. You might prefer wood, plastic, or even metal as a handle, and choosing your favorite will help. Check out the gardening store where you can feel out the shovels and figure out which ones feel suitable to you.

Wheelbarrows

A wheelbarrow might sound like overkill, but you will probably need to move large amounts of material around. You may have to move quantities of mulch or soil around to prepare and maintain your garden space. When you have a good wheelbarrow, you will be able to use it often. Wheelbarrows are especially useful in cleaning out, winterizing, and transporting materials to and from the garden. A wheelbarrow pays for itself several times over in utility and value.

Pots

Pots are a great way for you to start your garden as well, and depending upon how you choose to garden, it may be the only place that you will be growing it. Some people use pots for container gardening, meaning the plants are grown in individual pots instead of planting directly into the ground. This is a way that you can grow plants indoors, which works well in climates that have a short growing season. There is a wide range of different kinds of pots that you can use, based on the space requirements of what you are trying to grow. Pots are perfect if you are short on outdoor space, want to expand your native-soil garden, or want to move plants around to follow the sun.

Fertilizer

Fertilizer becomes essential, especially if you live somewhere that does not have very good soil. Depleted soil doesn't have the nutrients necessary to support healthy plant growth. Fertilizin products come in a wide range of nutrient levels and application methods, and it's vital to use them safely and correctly. We'll be taking a look at the effective use of fertilizers later in the book, but just keep in mind for now that this is something you'll likely be putting on your shopping list during the gardening season.

Starter Trays

Starter trays are perfect if you want to get a head start before you transplant your seedlings outdoors. By starting plants indoors, you reap the benefit of having plants ready to go as soon as it is warm enough to garden and being able to identify healthy and unhealthy seedlings before you waste time putting them in the ground. Started trays come in many forms, but most people are familiar with divided rectangular trays. You can also find individual pots, round trays for herbs and microgreens, and an assortment of environmentally-friendly compostable and plantable pots. You can also save up household items for starting seeds- milk jugs, soda bottles, and the like. If it's small and you can put a drain hole in the bottom and some potting soil into it, it can be a seed starter. Keep in mind that sprouting seeds need to be somewhere warm and sunny, or you'll have to provide them with a grow lamp.

Garden Soil

Healthy, aerated, fertile soil is the foundation of every successful garden. Soil is a living entity that needs regular care to maintain its nutrient balance. If you live in an area where the soil is notoriously rocky or barren, you'll have to amend your soil with fertilizers and organic material like compost before you can plant your vegetables. You may also need to add sand to loosen up clay soil, or clay to tighten up silt. A soil test done by an authorized laboratory is a great place to start learning what your land needs to heal and be ready to grow. You can contact your area's farm bureau or cooperative extension for more information on having a test done. The results will come with recommendations to fix your soil's pH, nutrient content, and composition as needed.

If you're going to be unable to amend your soil, you can consider raised bed and/or container gardening. These methods are great, but you're going to have to have soil imported to your property. When buying soil in bulk, only buy from qualified landscape suppliers who can give you a guarantee that the soil is clean, free of toxins, and has been tested for nutrient content. There is no sense in purchasing soil that will have to be amended anyway. When you have your soil delivered, be sure to secure a tarp over the pile if you can't get it distributed right away. You'll have a muddy mess and a lot of waste on your hands if it rains before you can attend to building your garden.

Hoe

A hoe is perfect if you are turning the soil to begin your garden or if you need to break up clumps of material. The sharp edge and leverage of a long handle make the hoe the ideal tools for these tasks. As with choosing a shovel that will work for you, you want to make sure that your hoe feels very comfortable in your hands.

Rake

There are two types of rakes to consider for your toolshed, the fanned leaf rake we're familiar with seeing in the fall and the straight-tined garden rake. Rakes are perfect for cleaning up the ground around your area and clearing out swaths in the garden. It would be best if you bought your rakes in person, like your shovels and hoes, to make sure that they feel comfortable in your hands.

Pitchfork

The humble pitchfork can be a workhorse when it comes to doing tough garden chores. Short-handled garden pitchforks can be used to turn tough soil, spread loads of straw and compost with ease, and dig up root vegetables at harvest time. Check out pitchforks in person to find one where the length and handle size is suited to your height and leverage.

Trowel

Hand trowels allow you to dig out soil in tight spaces and when you only need to create small holes. A trowel is going to be your go-to hand tool for transplanting seedlings and moving small amounts of soil. You can find trowels in several sizes and shapes, and they come in molded plastic or metal. Some trowels have a terrific feature on the blade, with measurements marked out so you can gauge your depth as you dig. This is useful when following planting recommendations for seed depth and spacing. The control you get from using a trowel lets you plant and transplant with ease without disturbing the other plants in the area.

Weed Puller

A weed puller, or weeding fork, is perfect if you want to get just the weeds and their roots out of the soil that you are moving. These tools resemble a large screwdriver with a forked end at the tip. That tip is inserted into the soil at the base of the weed, and you quickly give it a twist or a jerk, then pry it up. This motion allows you to then pull the weed loose without bothering any plants or roots around it.

Loppers

Loppers look like long-handled hedge trimmers, and these primarily come into play if you have trees or other thick vines that might be too much for regular gardening shears to handle. While this book is mainly focused on vegetable gardening, you may still find that these are useful for you, especially if you are clearing an undeveloped space for your garden or have thorny shrubs and vines on your property.

Gloves

Gardening gloves are essential for protecting your hands while you work. When you are building, digging, and hauling materials, a good pair of leather gloves can protect you from splinters, blisters, cuts, and scrapes. Keeping your hands covered also staves off infection or allergic reactions from soil pathogens and plant irritants. For regular gardening chores, find a cloth, leather, or synthetic material glove that fits well and protects your hands, wrists, and lower arms from being injured and accumulating too much dirt. You want to leave the soil in the garden, not under your fingernails.

Water Source

You need some sort of source for water for your garden. Whether you'll be doing so manually, build irrigation, or have some other methods of getting water to your plants. This means you'll need irrigation equipment like soaker or drip hoses, regular hoses, and/or watering cans. We'll discuss the importance of water again when we talk about siting your garden and maintaining it during the growing season.

Pruning Shears

Pruning shears are like the smaller version of loppers, and you're going to want a good sharp pair to trim and prune your plants. Sometimes, you'll have a plant that gets out of control and unwieldy, and pruning it back can tame it. Other times, you'll have plants that might be diseased or damaged-cutting off the damaged tissue can help the plant redirect its resources into its healthy parts to continue proper growth. Pruning shears are also useful for cleanly harvesting vine fruits and vegetables like those in the cucurbit family (cucumbers, squash, melons, pumpkins, etc.)

Kneeling Pad

A kneeling pad is another one of those self-explanatory tools. Made from thick foam rubber, kneeling pads allow you to get down close to your work without needing to put your knees directly on the hard ground. If you want to go one step further, there are some excellent combination stool/kneeler products on the market that are super comfortable and affordable. These allow you to sit or kneel comfortably no matter what your task entails.

Tool Storage

Once you've acquired all your tools and supplies, you don't want them to get ruined, so you will need some sort of storage system. There's no sense in spending time and money collecting your tools only to have them ruined by the weather, so figure out a way to keep them safe and dry. You can get an inexpensive composite tool shed or trunk or allot a space for your tools on a screened-in porch or mudroom. If you have other larger lawn equipment stowed in a garage or shed, you should be able to fit your gardening stuff alongside it as well.

Now that we've taken a good look at many of the tools and supplies you'll need to get started, let's discuss the big "whys" of gardening. In the next chapter, we'll talk about how you can make your garden work for you and why having a vegetable garden is beneficial in so many ways.

Chapter 3:
Can You Make Money
Growing Gardens at Home?

N ow, it's time to get down to what you're here to learn. It's time to consider what it would take for you to start earning money. Gardening can be a lucrative pursuit if you have the time and space to utilize. Growing veggies at home is an excellent way for you to make money, invest profits back into expanding your garden and spend time doing what you love. When it comes to monetizing your garden, you can take several different approaches, so let's take a look at an overview of those options and how you can make them work for you. Later in the book, we can dive into the nuts and bolts of becoming a profitable market gardener.

Not everyone is ready to take the leap into selling their vegetables for profit, and that's okay! Gardening has many significant benefits. It's good for your physical and mental health, provides your family with fresh, flavorful food, and it's a hobby that people of all ages and abilities can enjoy. But if you are interested in turning your veggies into cash, here are some terrific ideas that you can consider.

Selling Produce

The quickest way to make some money on your vegetables is by selling them, as is, after harvest. You can do this the old-fashioned way, with a produce stand at the end of your driveway, or you can look into wholesale and retail options. If you have the space to produce a large quantity or variety of vegetables, it may be worth your time and money to secure a stall at a farmer's market. You can even find a partner to split the stall costs. This is usually someone like you, who is just getting started, or a mentor or established market gardener that grows things that compliment, not compete with yours. If you can be prolific enough to produce large quantities of certain vegetables, you could even look into supplying small markets and restaurants through wholesale deals.

- farmer's markets are a terrific direct sales option for selling your produce -

The key to being successful at growing and selling fresh vegetables is to understand what people want. They are looking for high-quality, locally-grown produce, and they are willing to pay well for it, so keep an eye on market prices and sell your own goods accordingly. If you price too low, people may not think you've got a quality product for sale- or worse, they will buy everything, but you won't have made any money. If you price yourself too high, customers will go elsewhere to purchase. We'll spend more time on setting prices to make a profit later, but for now, just keep in mind that you want to keep your gardening expenses and other overhead costs low and price your goods accordingly to the fair market value. This is how you make money selling raw, fresh vegetables.

Knowing your market also means knowing what you can grow that will sell. Think about the basic economics that you learned in school. It's all about supply and demand, so you need to produce things that meet that demand. Popular items like cucumbers, tomatoes, and peppers are always a hit because everyone loves having these items in the summer. But also think about the other things people enjoy year-round. Lettuce can be grown from March to October in most climates, and other cool-weather crops can be cultivated at both the beginning and end of the warm growing season.

Selling Seeds

You can also sell seeds from your garden, which can be a hit at festivals, fairs, plant exchanges, and farmer's markets. People like to purchase seeds from proven stock, and if you're raising healthy, heirloom-variety plants, saving and selling the seeds can be a good source of side income. Saving seeds isn't terribly difficult, and packaging and labeling can be a simple and inexpensive as some tiny envelopes and self-print labels. Seed-selling is a terrific side niche, and it's a great way to sell value-added products during the off-season.

- simple, beautiful packaging can make your seeds more attractive to customers -

Selling Plants

You can also choose to sell seedlings and cuttings to people who prefer not to start their plants from seed. You don't have to plant a ton of extra seedlings for this to be a viable option. People who seek out seedlings and cuttings are looking for thriving young plants that they can transplant directly into their own gardens without any muss or fuss. If you are skilled at starting seedlings or propagating cuttings, this is definitely something to think about.

- raising extra seedlings for sale is a great way to make a little extra money -

Run a U-Pick Garden

If your town allows the zoning and you have enough space to accommodate visitors, you may be able to run a U-Pick garden. These are gardens where people come in person and pay a fee to choose the produce they want fresh directly from the plant. Many people love the experience of getting out and picking their own dinner, and you get the added benefit of selling your fruits and vegetables without having to be the one to harvest.

Begin a CSA or Subscription Service

A CSA, which stands for community-supported agriculture, is a service that people can sign up for every year to receive an assortment of fresh produce on a regular basis. CSAs or subscription produce services can work in a number of different ways. You can give customers options regarding how much produce they will get, such as small, medium, and large box options, and how frequently they will receive their items. Many market gardeners will also offer clients the chance to exclude items from their boxes that they absolutely won't eat because this eliminates food waste. However, the majority of people who sign up for CSAs or produce subscriptions are happy to receive whatever they get- it gives them an opportunity to expand their palates and try out new recipes.

While these are all fantastic ideas for monetizing a garden, no one is making any cash until you actually design, build, plant, and harvest, so let's move on to the real business at hand- being a gardener!

Part 2:

Building Your Garden

Chapter 4:
Location, Location, Location

When it comes time to start your garden, you have to have a game plan because your efforts aren't likely to be very effective without one. There's a popular phrase among horticulturalists- "the right plant in the right place"- and that's key when planning a garden. You want to give your vegetables the best possible living situation, which means access to the proper amount of sun, air, and water, and healthy, fertile soil

If you've never designed or planted a garden before, now's your chance to learn. Choosing a good location is a combination of common sense and knowing what plants need to grow and thrive. Location can make all the difference in the quality of your garden's produce. Within this chapter, we'll be going over the components that make up an ideal garden space, so you can look around your property and choose what's going to work best for you. A great location goes a long way towards a thriving, successful gardening experience.

What Makes a Good Garden Space?

The best garden spaces are close enough for convenient access but are far enough away to be safe from regular foot traffic. They should also ensure that all of the plants' needs are met. When you look at your space, you have to look at everything that it has to offer. How much sunlight does it get? What is the general shape of your land? Are there any obstructions or slopes that might create a run-off problem or block the sun? The best gardens are the ones that check off all the major criteria.

Even better, your garden space is more effective if you think about organization. Do you have a specific design in mind? Will traditional rows work best for you, or would you prefer to have several small beds instead? Are you going to be tilling the native soil or building raised beds to accommodate your need? You can even get creative about round shapes like spirals and mounds, depending on your landscape and available materials. Gardens don't have to be boring- they can reflect your personal tastes and work preferences while still maximizing your space.

One of the best ways to choose an appropriate garden site is to be an observer. If you're debating between a few different locations, take some time to see what happens in those spaces when it rains and when it's sunny. Where does the water go when it rains? If it pools where you want to build a garden, that might be a location to be wary about- you don't want to drown out your plants. If this is also the location that gets the most sunlight, it might be worth fixing the drainage with some inexpensive channeling.

The thing is, there is rarely such a thing as a "perfect" garden site unless you're willing to clear trees, level property, and otherwise dump a lot of resources into creating one. For most people, it's best to make do with what you have and base your decision on observation and a cost-benefit analysis of making significant changes to your landscape.

Choosing the right location really is as simple as evaluating the various parts of your property to figure out what space will work best for the plants you intend to grow. It helps not to overcomplicate things, so we've made a list of criteria that you should be considering- it should help make your decision a bit easier.

How much sun is in your area?

First and foremost, you need to observe how the sunlight falls in the area that you are thinking about for your garden. As we discussed, most vegetable plants prefer full sun, which means eight or more hours a day. This just isn't feasible for many people, but you still need to choose a site with a minimum of six hours of sunlight. Otherwise, your plants won't take in enough energy to photosynthesize, and their growth will be stunted. Plants that require full or partial shade can be planted under larger plants and at the shady margins of your gardening area to satisfy their needs.

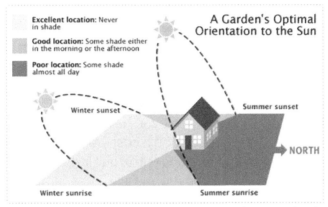

Excellent location: Never in shade

Good location: Some shade either in the morning or the afternoon

Poor location: Some shade almost all day

A Garden's Optimal Orientation to the Sun

Winter sunset

Summer sunset

NORTH

Winter sunrise

Summer sunrise

- being an observer will help you choose the best location for your garden -

How saturated is your soil?

We've already talked about the importance of delivering just the right amount of water to your garden. Too much, and the roots will drown or be smothered, and they won't be able to hold your plants in place or adequately perform gas and nutrient exchange. You want to site your garden somewhere where erosion, run-off, and standing water won't be a problem. The best locations for vegetable gardens are level places where the soil retains natural moisture but doesn't get swampy or oversaturated. This means you'll need to make sure the soil has good drainage or amended to improve its drainage qualities. Plants that prefer wetter soil can be placed at the bottom of any gentle slopes, and those that like to stay a bit drier should be planted on higher ground or elevated in well-drained containers.

- places where water pools like this aren't ideal for a vegetable garden; you'll need a channel to divert the water, or you can choose a different location –

How close is the garden to your source of water?

Even if you've chosen a spot with the perfect natural soil saturation, you'll still need to provide your plants with water. Think about it- do you want to drag hoses or schlep watering cans across your entire property, or do you want to build your garden close to a water source? I think we all know the answer to that! Consider where your water comes from when you're considering where you want your garden to grow. It will save you a lot of time and energy in the long run. Plus, it's tough to get motivated when you have to haul water. Even with the best intentions, you'll fall into a pattern of underwatering because it's just too tedious.

How busy is the area you are gardening in?

If you try to set up your garden where all of the kids go running around or where your dogs go digging, they're probably not going to be suitable places. The sweet spot in gardening is finding a happy medium between having the garden close enough to your house, so you don't have to hike for miles just to harvest some tomatoes, and having it far enough away from regular activity so that your kids and pets don't go traipsing through and trample your plants. You can also think about areas that are easy to put a wire or wooden fence around; this helps with domestic "intrusion" as well as with keeping out curious wildlife.

Is there some sort of structure that will impact growth in your location?

Some things will actively make your gardening process more difficult. When you're in the planning stages, look around at the spaces you want to use and observe if there are any obstructions. Will your house cast a shadow as the sun moves? Are there any large trees that might throw too much shade in the middle of summer? These are important observations to make before you plant a single seed.

Another factor in planning your gardens near existing structures is a phenomenon known as a heat island effect. Concrete patios, brick walls, and even wooden buildings retain heat during the day and radiate it out when the air around them becomes cooler. Although we see this more in urban settings, a stone patio can wreak havoc on a countryside garden. In some colder climates, this effect is desirable and can be harnessed to keep plants warm in less-than-ideal growing conditions. It's best in most temperate climates to avoid planting directly next to brick and stone- plants need the cool, dark evenings to rest and recuperate. Too much heat can cause wilting and invite pests and pathogens.

Matching Plants to the Right Places

Plants do best when they are settled into places that make them happy. This means giving them everything they need to the best of your ability. Stick to plants that are suited for growing in your climate. When you choose seeds and seedlings, they will be marked with their appropriate growing zone. Plant tags and seed labels also include what conditions that particular plant prefers, taking all the guesswork out of cultivation. These little tags are a wealth of information, giving you the planting instructions, space/water/light requirements, and the mature plant's approximate size. All this data gives you the knowledge you need to always put your plants in the best position to succeed. You can use this information to design and organize your garden to provide each plant the optimal growing conditions.

Given all the information we've gone over in this chapter, you've probably got a good idea about where you're going to be putting your garden. Take the time to observe your property and choose the best location to suit your needs. It's a good idea to take a tape measure outside with you and write down your thoughts and measurements as they come to you. Once you've decided on *where* you're going to build, the next step is to decide *how* you're going to build. Let's head on over to the next chapter and talk about your options.

Chapter 5:
Prepping and Building Your Garden with Profit in Mind

When you have chosen your garden location, it's time to start working on your complete design and plan. There are a few stages to this, and working on them in order will make your building, planning, and maintenance a lot easier in the long run. When you work on your garden plan, you will need to start making a few decisions. Will you be constructing raised beds, or are you going to work directly in your native soil? You also need to decide if your land needs leveling before you begin building in earnest.

This is when you need to break out a pencil, paper, and ruler and start sketching some designs. It's always easier to erase and start over than it is to undo a bunch of digging, so draw up a few different plans and decide which you like best. It's also a great idea to keep a garden journal, so when you're done with your designs, you can tuck them into a notebook (or scan them into a computer if you're more of a digital journalist) for reference if you need to revisit them. Draw dimensions, pencil in where you're thinking about installing each type of plant, and mark where important structures and facilities are, like your water supply or any tall trees. Let's go over your options for building your garden, so you've got the knowledge you need to start designing.

Choosing Garden Beds or Ground for Gardening

When it comes to growing your plants, one of the first choices you will need to make is determining whether you want to grow your garden in garden beds or directly in the soil. They each have their benefits, and ultimately, it comes down to personal preference to determine which to use.

Garden beds

A garden bed, also commonly called a raised bed, resembles a sandbox, but for gardening. Raised beds sit above the ground and are typically built to a height of six to eight inches. If you are designing and constructing raised garden beds for yourself, you can customize the depth to suit your needs, but keep in mind that your plants' roots will need room to grow down into the soil. A depth of fewer than 6 inches is not recommended. As long as you factor in drainage, raised beds can be constructed from almost any material that will contain soil. You can purchase pre-fabricated kits in wood, composite, or PVC vinyl if you're not particularly handy. These kits come in a variety of sizes, styles, and price points.

-raised bed gardens are good for places where digging in the native soil is untenable; they also offer better drainage and higher soil temperature -

If you are going to construct your beds from scratch, think about where you can get materials that won't blow your budget. Check out local marketplace sites and see if anyone is selling leftover wood, bricks, or stone. Contact any friends you have in the contracting trades to see if they've got any surplus you can have for cheap or free. One note of caution- don't use pressure-treated lumber to build garden beds for producing food. The chemicals used to treat the wood can leach into your soil and create toxicity, and no one wants to spend time and money growing food that isn't safe for consumption.

When you're designing raised garden beds, size does matter. Anything more than six feet wide makes it hard to work in the beds without stepping into them, and anything more than eight feet long becomes unwieldy when you're building and moving the frames. The most popular dimensions for raised beds fall between three and six feet wide and four and eight feet long, with depths between 12 and 24 inches. The taller the bed, the easier it is on the back, but the more soil you'll have to import to fill them. That's the trade-off.

Separating the garden bed from the native soil provides a number of benefits:

- **Easier to manage:** Having raised beds means less bending and twisting and more freedom to plant in clusters (so you can have more plants per square footage).
- **Weed control:** High-quality imported soil should be certified free of weed seed when you purchase it.
- **Preventing soil compaction:** Soil compaction is a real issue in native soil gardens, but since raised beds are not walked on, the problem is alleviated or eliminated.

- **Plant protection:** Plants in raised beds are less likely to be trampled.
- **Extended growing season:** Because the soil in raised beds warms up quicker and retains more heat, it allows you to lengthen your growing period. Soil held above the ground is generally warmer than the average ground temperature.
- **Less maintenance:** Because the soil in your raised bed is stable and is not going to compact, making it less likely to attract weeds, you have less maintenance to worry about with these gardens. Weeds are more prevalent in soil that has been disturbed.
- **Better drainage:** Raised beds tend to drain better than the soil at ground level because they are elevated. If you live somewhere that tends to get massive amounts of rainfall, you may find better success with raised beds to avoid drowning your roots.

Growing in the soil

If you choose to grow directly in the soil, you have other benefits to consider instead. It's recommended that you get a soil test before planting, as this will tell you if you need to make any amendments or enrichments before planting. At the very least, you might want to add some compost to increase organic matter in the soil- you can literally never have too many living organisms in your soil. In addition to not having to go through the time and expense of building raised beds, the other benefits of using your native soil are:

- **You don't have to get more soil:** When you choose a raised bed, you have to purchase soil and fill the beds. Gardening directly in your native soil eliminates this expanse and time-consuming chore.
- **Less work to start:** Because you don't have to build anything, you can prepare your plot with just a tiller or a tractor and then start growing. Tillers are usually available to rent by the day, so you don't even have to worry about the expense of purchasing one!
- **Easier to irrigate:** Your flat garden will also be more accommodating, should you choose to use an irrigation system. The fewer joints and moving parts you have, the less opportunity there will be for leaks and breaks.

- traditional row gardens should leave space to work between the rows for weeding, harvesting, and watering -

Native soil gardening has its downsides, as well. As we previously mentioned, weeds tend to spring up wherever the soil is disturbed- and the act of tilling is an act of disturbance. Native soil gardens are also more prone to wind and water erosion, so soil health is of the utmost importance. We'll talk a lot more about how to keep your soil healthy when we discuss compost, mulch, and weed control later on. Choosing what type of garden to build is mostly a personal choice. If you've got rocky, untillable soil, then you may need to jump straight into raised bed gardening. Many people choose based on their physical abilities. Raised beds are more accessible to those with mobility concerns. The wonderful thing about starting a garden from scratch, though, is that you can weigh your personal preferences against the physical properties of your space and soil to make the decision that's right for you.

Build Your Garden

Let's lay out all your design, planning, and building steps in order, so you've got a checklist of garden creation. When you follow the list, you'll be ensuring that things go smoothly and you don't miss anything. There's never any sense in having to backtrack and accidentally make more work for yourself.

Step 1: Choose your location

The first step of building your dream garden is to figure out where to put it. Using the criteria and the observational points we discussed earlier in this chapter, you'll be able to find the best spot on your property to begin construction.

Step 2: Draw your design(s)

Once you've chosen your location, it's time to take some measurements and take your pencil to paper. Draw up some designs that will work inside the space you have. Don't forget to mark crucial elements like your water source, and be sure your sketches leave room for things like walkways. Have fun with it. If you don't want to have a boring rectangular garden, then don't! Round beds, spirals, and four-squares are also terrific design choices, and you can always add space to pop a birdbath or bench. You are going to spend a lot of time working in your garden, so go ahead and make it an area that's comfortable and inviting.

Step 3: Planning and building the beds

When you have a finalized design, you're going to need a materials list (if you're building raised beds, don't forget nice sturdy hardware!). Make sure you have *everything* you need before you begin. There is nothing more frustrating than having to stop halfway through a project to run out to the hardware store or lumberyard. If you're tilling your gardens in the ground, some inexpensive stakes and twine will go a long way towards guiding you; mark out the dimensions of your planned beds *before* you fire up the tiller.

Herbs
basil
cilantro
Dill
Oregano
mint
rosemary
Sage
thyme
parsley
sorrel

Greens
lettuce
Spinach
Swiss chard
Arugala

Brassicas
Brocolli
Brussel sprouts
cabbage
kale

Solanums
peppers
tomatoes

Legumes
bush beans
pole snap beans
runner beans

Runner Beans

Assorted Lettuces

Morning Glories

Roots
Beets
Carrots
potatoes
radishes

Curcurbits
cucumbers
squashes

- whether you draw by hand or use a computer application, designing your garden before you plant is a crucial step –

Step 4: Preparing the soil

If you haven't already gotten your soil tested, now is the time! And if you're buying soil in bulk to fill raised beds, you should be ready to have that delivered once you get your beds built. Be sure to purchase soil only from a trusted garden center or supplier. They can help you determine the yardage you need based on the dimensions of your beds. For extra drainage, order a small quantity of coarse gravel or quarry-process (QP) stone to put as a base layer in your beds before adding the soil.

- a sample soil test kit; you can get these from your local farm bureau or Cooperative Extension-

You want your soil to be moist, clump-free, and clear of rocks and obstructions. Add compost, if you can, to begin increasing organic matter. Tiny organisms like microbes and fungus are crucial to the health of your soil and your garden. They're integral to the life cycle of your plants, so feed them with lots of compost, and you'll have a happier garden. Remember, soil = living, dirt = dead.

When you have soil delivered, try to get it installed the same day. If you must leave it overnight, cover it securely, lest it rains and washes away some of your investment. We know we already said this, but it bears repeating. It is always better to avoid a muddy mess.

Step 5: Installing irrigation

If you are going to be installing soaker hoses or drip irrigation, the best time to lay that out and hook it up is BEFORE you plant. It's so much easier to see where the hoses go, run the water to test the system, and see where the water goes when there aren't any plants in the way. If you're not going to be using an irrigation system, you should at least hook up your hose and walk it around your empty garden to make sure it reaches everywhere it needs to go. If not, invest in a longer hose or an extension before you plant. A high-quality nozzle with several force settings is never a bad investment, either.

Are Greenhouses Worth It?

That question pretty much says it all. People want to know if a greenhouse is a worthwhile investment, which is a pretty personal choice. Greenhouses come in a wide assortment of styles, and they are priced according to construction materials and features. If you are interested in greenhouse gardening and want to know if the benefits are worth the cost, think about why you'd like to have one.

Greenhouses are used for two main purposes: to extend the growing season for plants native to a region that has a naturally short season and to grow species that aren't suited for the natural environment of your climate. The first is the most prevalent use of a home greenhouse; if you live in the northern United States or Canada, a greenhouse can protect your plants and let you enjoy them long enough to get to harvest. They also allow room and resources to get seeds started without taking up space inside your home. For growing things that aren't suited to your climate zone, you would need a temperature-controlled greenhouse, also referred to as a hothouse. If you live in Toronto and want to grow hibiscus and orchids, you'll likely need a hothouse to do so.

The bottom line here comes down to how much you are willing to invest and where you live. If you live somewhere like the southern United States, where the weather is usually warm enough to grow nearly year-round, you probably don't need a greenhouse. They can be cost-prohibitive, too. A permanent, tempered-glass greenhouse can cost somewhere in the range of $20,000. Smaller do-it-yourself models can cost much, much less, but it takes a lot of time to build and maintain them. You get, as they say, what you pay for.

Many commercial growers swear by greenhouses thanks to the power that they have to keep the gardens warm and producing. However, this might be something that's best served for you later on, after you've had the chance to start building that income up. Once you start getting the money in, you can consider whether this sort of permanent fixture is in the cards for you.

Part 3:

Planting Your Garden

Chapter 6:
Starting Your Plants

You can't grow a garden without any plants, so that begs the question- how are you going to acquire them? You have several options available to you to populate your vegetable patch, and what you use will depend on your comfort and skill levels. This chapter will take a close look at starting from seed and using seedlings and plant starts. We'll also give you an overview of how cuttings work so that you can think about that as an option in the future. The idea is to figure out how to get the healthiest plants possible before you even put them in the garden.

There are pros and cons to each method of plant propagation, but we're going to walk you through the processes so you can make an informed decision about what's going to work best for you. Once you have a deeper understanding of a plant's life cycle, how to choose seeds and seedlings, read seed packets and plant tags to interpret growing requirements, and how to cultivate your seeds, seedlings, and cuttings, you'll have a good foundation for gardening success.

The Life Cycle of Plants

Plants, like people, go through a series of changes as they grow from seed to mature plant. Most vegetable species are annuals, which means they complete their entire life cycle from seed through die-off in a single growing season. When thinking about the life cycle of a plant, it's important to remember that the plant has a single purpose, and that is to reproduce. Plants are genetically programmed to create their own next generation, and they do this by producing flowers and fruit. When we harvest our vegetables, we're interrupting the plant's natural life cycle to take what we need from them. Let's start with the seed and what happens when we plant them to understand how the process begins.

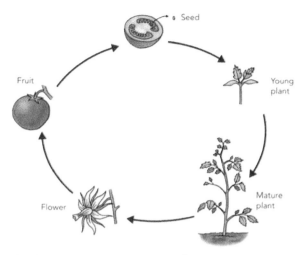

- the life cycle of a tomato plant –

Seeds

Seeds are an integral part of the reproductive system of a plant. The seed itself is the tissue enclosed in the tough exterior known as the seed casing. This tissue is the plant's embryo containing the genetic material the species needs to grow into the next generation of plants. Seed are classified into two categories- heirloom and hybrid. Heirloom seeds are from varieties that carry the same genetic code as the previous plant. They will grow into a copy of the plant that produced the seed. Heirloom species are essential for preserving history through agriculture and are proven varieties that have set characteristics. Hybrid seeds are for plant varieties that have been cross-bred to enhance desirable traits and eliminate unwanted ones. There is no guarantee that a plant grown from seeds saved from a hybrid will behave in the same way as its parent plant. If you remember your high school biology lessons, you'll likely remember Punnett squares to determine genetic probabilities. Hybrid plant species function in this manner. You don't know precisely what you'll get from generation to generation.

When you're planting a home garden or market garden, choosing heirloom or hybrid varieties is a personal choice, but there are benefits to each to consider. Heirloom varieties have few surprises. You get the exact plant you expect to have, and you can save seeds from an heirloom plant to grow that species again the following season. The downside to heirloom plants is that they are not as resistant to pests and pathogens as hybrid varieties. That's the upside to the hybrid varieties; they are bred specifically to avoid the common problems that plague their heirloom cousins. However, because they are genetically crossed, it's not recommended to save seeds from hybrid plants. Many of them are sterile, and the seeds that *can* reproduce cannot be guaranteed to exhibit the most desirable traits.

Germination

Germination is the next step in the life cycle of a plant. This stage is characterized by the rupture of the seed casing and the emergence of the seedling. You can germinate seeds in a couple of different ways, but the most crucial component to germination is moisture. Seeds can be germinated directly in soil, and this is effective only when they've been planted at the correct depth, are kept in a warm place, and the soil is evenly, consistently moist. Germination time in soil varies by plant species, but it generally takes anywhere from a few days to a couple of weeks to see a seedling emerge from the soil.

Another way to stimulate germination is to soak the seeds before placing them in your soil. You can do this by wrapping the seeds in a dampened paper towel, placing the towel in a bag, and placing it somewhere warm. Check on the seeds every day, and transplant them into soil as soon as the seedling emerges from the seed casing. If you leave the seeds wrapped in a wet towel for too long, they can mold and rot. Understanding the germination process is crucial if you intend to start your garden indoors before the outdoor growing season.

Seedlings
Seedlings are the beginning of the growth of the plant. If the seed is an embryo and the germination process is akin to gestation, then the seedling is the newborn plant. Seedlings require a lot of attention to their needs to mature correctly, just like an infant. Seedlings have to be able to grow in two directions- roots into the soil and leaves and stem

into the air- so they require loose, evenly moist soil to take hold of and light and airflow for proper upward development.

When seedlings emerge, they have their first tender leaves. These leaves need to be treated with care because they will be performing the plant's early photosynthesis. Make sure that your seedlings are in a safe, warm place and have at least 8 hours of direct light every day to ensure steady growth. Getting off to a good start is the best way to have plenty of healthy plants for your garden.

Mature Plant

The plant will continue to develop leaves and grow taller until it is large enough to perform enough photosynthesis to support itself. The roots will also settle down into the soil and extend themselves to draw up water and nutrients. When a plant has reached maturity, it will flower. For some plants, the flower will blossom, be fertilized, and grow the fruit you will harvest. For other plants, you'll be stopping the life cycle before flowering. These are things that you are growing specifically for the leaves, like lettuce and some brassica vegetables, but you can always let one or two plants bolt purposely if you'd like to save the seeds. Once these veggies have flowered (called bolting), the leaves will have become bitter and inedible.

Flowering and Pollination

Flowers contain the plant's reproductive organs, and if you want your plants to bear fruit, the flowers will need to be pollinated. Inside each flower is the ovary, and for it to be fertilized, it needs pollen to be brought to it. Very few home garden vegetables are wind-pollinated, which means your garden will have to rely on insect pollinators like bees, wasps, butterflies, and moths. Hummingbirds are also excellent pollinators if they are native to your area. Pollination occurs when pollinators land on a flower to drink nectar. The pollen gets stuck to their bodies and legs and is carried to the next plant they stop at. The pollen then travels down the pistol and stamen (the protrusions you see in the center of a flower) into the ovary to fertilize the plant.

Fruiting

The fruit is the product of a fertilized flower, and for many of the plants we consider vegetables, the fruit is the part we consume. Fruit is the term for the seed-bearing portion of a plant, and its job is to protect the seeds until they can self-sow and create the next generation. Again, we interrupt the life cycle by harvesting the fruit before dropping, decomposing, and depositing the seeds into the soil. Most tomato gardeners will tell you that they've had fruit drop before it could be harvested, and the following year, they'll have random tomato plants popping up. Of course, species like tomatoes, cucumbers and squash, peppers, eggplant, and many others are technically fruits, not vegetables. What we consume from each plant in our garden varies, and many are multi-purpose. If you grow beets, the root is considered the main harvest vegetable, but the beet-tops (the greens) are delicious and full of nutrients, too.

Death or Dormancy

Once plants have expended their energy to bear flowers, fruit, and seeds, their life cycle comes to either an end or enters dormancy. The vast majority of vegetable plants are annuals, so they will only survive for one season. Some herbs and root vegetables are biennials or perennials, which means they will return for two or more growing seasons. Once the plants die off, you should compost any that do not have any signs of pest damage or pathogens. The material will break down over the winter, and you can mix it back into your soil in the spring to provide nutrients.

Starting from Seeds

If you are starting some of your plants indoors, you'll have to understand the full process of starting from seed. We talked briefly about supplies earlier in the book and just a little way back about the process of germination. Not all plants can be started indoors, and not all seeds that are started indoors need to be soaked and germinated in damp paper towels. This information will be found on your seed packets, so read them carefully.

The most commonly used method of indoor seed starting is to use seedling trays. These can be found inexpensively online or anywhere that retails garden supplies. Seedling trays are made up of rows of connected plastic cells that hold your soil or other starter media. You can even find some that have clear lids to turn your trays into tiny tabletop greenhouses. These are terrific for keeping your soil warm and moist while your seeds germinate. You don't have to use a seedling tray, though- recycled materials work just as well. You can save plastic water and juice bottles, milk cartons or jugs, or use disposable cups. As long as you have good quality potting soil and some receptacles, you're all set to start your seeds indoors. You'll also need a sunny spot, or a grow light to nurture your seedlings once they emerge. Labeling your seedlings is always a good idea, too. You can use popsicle sticks or plastic spoons for this- just write the plant's name onto them with a permanent marker and stick them into the side of the seedling cell.

- seedlings started indoors will have a great head start when it's time to transplant into the garden -

Many seedling trays have their drain holes on the bottom and come with a second solid tray to nest into. This is to facilitate a technique known as bottom-watering, and it's helpful so you don't overwater your soil and cause your seeds to mold or rot before they can germinate and sprout. If you don't use commercial seedling trays, you can still use bottom-watering to start your seeds. Simply put drain holes in the bottom of your recycled material seed-pots, and set them into an old baking pan or inexpensive shallow storage tub. To bottom-water your seedling trays, all you have to do is place a small amount of water in the pan or nesting tray each day. The water will be drawn up by the wicking effect through the drain holes and into the soil as needed.

Once your seedlings have sprouted, make sure they stay consistently warm and have light at least eight hours a day. As they grow, you'll be able to see which seedlings are thriving and which might not be as healthy. It's okay to cull out unsuccessful seedlings. You don't need to transplant them into the garden and have them fail. That's why it's important to plant more seedlings than you will need for transplantation. You don't have to feel guilty about removing any unhealthy plants, and you may even have some seedlings left over for sale.

For the best results with starting seeds indoors, be sure to follow the planting instructions on your seed packets. They will tell you how deep to plant the seeds, how much light and water they need and give you a timetable for starting indoors and when to transplant. Seed packets also provide you with spacing requirements and other outdoor cultivation data, so don't throw them away. Tuck them into your garden journal, or if you're the digital sort, take photos of them and upload them to your garden files.

Note: If you're not a fan of plastic seedling trays, you can use biodegradable pots, which cost a bit more, but can be planted directly into the soil with the seedlings in them, after which the pots decompose. For a less alternative to this, you can use cardboard egg cartons. These types of materials cannot be bottom-watered, though, for obvious reasons, so you'll have to be extra vigilant to keep them evenly watered without having the materials disintegrate before you're ready to transplant.

Starting from Seedlings

Starting from seedlings is probably the most straightforward method for getting your garden planted and growing. When you source seedlings, you want to shop around plants that look healthy and sturdy. Make sure you get instructions with your seedlings. Most commercial growers will have plant tags stuck into each pot, and private growers should be able to give you the information you need about spacing, watering, light, and other cultivation requirements. Don't buy potted seedlings too far ahead of transplant time. You should be able to install the plant in your garden within a few days of purchase, or you run the risk of the seedlings drying out, wilting, or getting root-bound into their pots. Always transplant seedlings into their permanent location in your garden. You don't want to have to disturb the roots by moving them again. We'll talk more about how to transplant correctly a little bit later in the book. This information will apply to both seedlings you've grown at home and ones you've acquired elsewhere.

Starting from Cuttings

Cloning plants is another method that you can use to grow your garden. This is achieved by taking a cutting from an existing healthy plant and forcing it to root. These plants will be genetically identical to the original plants. It's a good way to know precisely what you're getting before you plant. You can use this method to sustain plants you already have or find another gardener to lend you some cuttings.

Cuttings have the benefit of bypassing the early stages of plant development. You don't have to wait for the plant to germinate, sprout, and mature. Most plants rooted from cuttings will mature and bear fruit fairly quickly, given the proper methods are used. Cloning a plant is simple; you just have to know where to take the cutting. Most gardeners prefer to take cuttings of strong, healthy branches near the base of the plant. These branches will have the most vascular material, which is vital for circulating water and nutrients through the plant. Lower branches also are closer to the source of the hormones that produce the rooting response and may still carry these in residual levels.

Once you've chosen a branch, the next step is to carefully and cleanly remove it from the parent plant. You should do this with the cleanest, sharpest clipper possible, or even an Exacto knife or similar scalpel blade if you have one. You want to make the cut flush down the main stem and then trim the end of the cut branch at a 45-degree angle. You can then dip the cut end into a little liquid fertilizer and place it in a vessel of potting soil, or put a few drops of liquid fertilizer in a glass or vase, fill it up with water, and set your cutting into the solution. After a few days, you will see root fibers emerging from the cutting. When these root fibers are long enough to sustain themselves in soil, you can transplant the cutting into the garden.

If you took the branch from one of your own plants, you need to keep an eye on the "wound" where you removed the cutting. Plants have an incredible ability to self-heal, but they can get infected wounds the same as humans. If you used a clean blade and made a proper cut, things should be fine, but it still always pays to be vigilant. If you made the cut correctly, you might see a couple of days of weeping (which should be clear or milky, never dark), and then you'll see the plant start to close us and form a scar. If you see insects attacking the cutting site, wash them off with cool water, pat the area dry, and gently wrap the wound with some wide floral tape for a day or two. If you see signs of infection, like dark oozing, clean the area every day, but do not wrap it! You don't want to trap the infection inside and further damage the plant.

That's if for this section- you've learned about the most common propagation methods for home gardeners! In the next few chapters, we're going to catalog some popular plant choices so you can start thinking about what you'd like to plant and how those plants can fit into your garden space. When we're done with those chapters, it'll be time to get down to the business of planting, maintaining, and troubleshooting your garden. Let's go!

Chapter 7:
Planting Full Shade
Vegetables

F irst, let's go over some vegetables that do well in full shade. If you live in an area with a short growing season, these are great options for planting in the early spring and late summer into fall, when the days are shorter. You don't have to worry about these varieties because they are also tolerant to cooler temperatures. This is also a terrific way to maximize your garden space. By growing cool weather shade-lovers early in the spring, they can be cultivated and harvested by the time you need space for your summer veggies. Then you can raise a second crop later in the year once the heat- and sun-loving plants have started to die off. These plants do well with about four hours of sunlight each day.

- leaf lettuces are great crops for growing at the beginning and end of each season -

Leaf Lettuce

What to Know: Leaf lettuce is a spring and fall crop that prefers cooler weather. In particular, you want to have 60-70 degree weather, and some varieties can be ready to harvest in just 30 days.

Water Requirements: Every few days, enough to dampen and surround the roots

Soil pH: 6 to 6.5

Best Varieties: Green leaf, red ruby

Best Companions: Garlic or Chives

Avoid Planting With: Nightshades like tomatoes or peppers

Space: 4" apart in rows 12" apart

Planting Depth: ½ inch

Harvest: When the leaves are full-sized. It can be harvested as leaves or as the full head.

Special Considerations: This will bolt if it gets too much light and will become bitter. Be mindful, and if it bolts, it is no longer suitable for eating but can be used for harvesting seeds.

Rutabagas

What to Know: Plant this plant early to mid-summer, depending upon your zone. It should be planted around three months before the first frost date.

Water Requirements: High water requirement—likes consistent ad constant water.

Soil pH: 5.5 – 7.0

Best Varieties: American Purple Top

Best Companions: Peas and onions

Avoid Planting with: Brassicas or mustard greens

Spacing: 6" to 8" apart in rows 12" to 18" apart

Planting Depth: ½", lightly covered and well-watered

Harvest: 90 days after planting or after the first or second frost. Cold weather improves the flavor.

Special Considerations: When the weather is too hot, it will taste bitter. Plant to harvest early spring or fall. If you live somewhere warmer in the southern climates, you can plant some just before the first frost and get a harvest in the late spring or early summer, but you don't want to let the plants grow in the summer, or they won't taste good.

Chapter 8: Planting Partial Sunlight Vegetables

While many vegetables require full sun, there are those that thrive on a little bit less sunshine, around 4-6 hours a day. Some of these are cool-weather plants that will do well with planting at the beginning and end of your growing season.

Arugula

What to Know: Arugula is a popular salad green, and it grows well in partial or full sun. It can be planted twice in a season for a late spring and an early fall harvest. Arugula matures quickly. Arugula should be sown directly in the soil because the delicate roots make it difficult to transplant successfully.

Water Requirements: Arugula, and most greens, prefer evenly moist, well-drained soil

Soil pH: 6.5 to 7

Best Varieties: Runway, Italian Rocket

Best Companions: Onions, Garlic

Avoid Planting With: Nightshades like tomatoes and peppers

Spacing: 1" between seeds, 10" between rows

Planting Depth: ¼" deep, covered lightly with soil

Harvest: As early as four weeks after planting

Special Considerations: You can harvest arugula continuously by planting new seeds every two-three weeks. Plant summer crops of arugula in the shadier part of your garden to avoid sunscald.

Beets

What to Know: Beets are another crop that you can get two harvests of in one season by planting early in the spring and later in the summer for a fall crop. Beet seeds should always be sown directly in the soil.

Water Requirements: evenly moist, well-drained soil; beets don't like to be too wet

Soil pH: 5.5 to 7

Best Varieties: Detroit Dark Red, Touchstone Gold

Best Companions: Lettuces

Avoid Planting With: Pole beans

Spacing: 1" to 2" apart, with 1' foot between rows

Planting Depth: ½" deep, cover lightly with soil

Harvest: 65-80 days, depending on the variety

Special Considerations: Beets are hardy, and a little bit of frost won't affect their growth. Don't forget that you can eat the beet tops (the greens) raw or cooked, as well.

Broccoli

What to Know: Broccoli loves cooler weather and the oblique sun of late spring and early fall. Make sure you leave lots of space for broccoli to spread and grow luscious, densely-packed heads.

Water Requirements: Broccoli is a thirsty crop; make sure it stays evenly, deeply watered

Soil pH: 5.5 to 7

Best Varieties: Green Goliath, Flash

Best Companions: Spinach, Onions

Avoid Planting With: Squash, Tomatoes

Spacing: 3" apart, with 3' between rows

Planting Depth: ½" if sowing outdoors, ¼" if sowing indoors

Harvest: 80 days

Special Considerations: You should always cut your broccoli heads before they begin to flower, as the longer they stay on the plant, the more bitter they will become.

Brussels Sprouts

What to Know: Brussels sprouts do very well in raised beds and other well-drained soils. They can be planted very early if started indoors so that they can enjoy a long growing season.

- Brussels sprouts are not only delicious but offer an interesting plant for your garden aesthetics -

Water Requirements: Brussels sprouts are thirsty but do not like being soggy. Keep soil evenly moist.

Soil pH: 6.5- 7

Best Varieties: Oliver, Churchill

Best Companions: Onions, cucumbers

Avoid Planting With: Tomatoes

Spacing: Seedlings should be placed 12" to 24" inches apart, seeds 6" to 12" then thinned

Planting Depth: ¼" deep, covered lightly and well-watered

Harvest: After 80 days, from the bottom up; whole stalks can also be pulled and hung upside down to preserve sprouts until ready to use

Special Considerations: Brussels sprouts are susceptible to mold issues due to the tight spaces in the heads of the sprouts. Make sure not to water the sprouts themselves, only the roots. Dry sprouts are happy sprouts.

Bush Tomatoes

What to Know: Bush tomatoes will do well just about anywhere, but for tight spaces, they are perfect in containers or raised beds and don't require as much staking as vine tomatoes, although small tomato cages will help your bush tomatoes stay upright when they get heavy with fruit.

Water Requirements: Tomatoes are among the thirstiest plants in the garden. Water them often and deeply.

Soil pH: 6-7

Best Varieties: Early Girl, Best Boy, San Marzano

Best Companions: Peas, beans, onions

Avoid Planting With: Peppers, potatoes

Spacing: 18" to 24"

Planting Depth: 1/2", lightly covered and well-watered

Harvest: Varies by variety, but 65-75 days average

Special Considerations: Bush tomatoes can be kept in pots and moved around to follow the sun. Just be mindful and cage them when they become heavy with fruit, and make sure any containers are well-drained and sturdy.

Cabbage

What to Know: Cabbage can be planted in the early spring and late summer for two crops but should always be directly sown. It is difficult to transplant their delicate roots.

Water Requirements: Soil should be evenly moist, never swampy

Soil pH: 6.5-7

Best Varieties: Stonehead, Gonzales, Cheers

Best Companions: Potatoes, cucumbers

Avoid Planting With: Tomatoes

Spacing: 12" to 24" apart, in rows 12" apart

Planting Depth: ¼" deep, lightly covered

Harvest: When heads are full and outer leaves just begin to curl open, 60-75 days by variety

Special Considerations: Cabbages are heavy feeders, so be sure to fertilize before planting and side-dress during the season.

Carrots

What to Know: Carrots need to have deep, loamy soil with lots of aeration and drainage to be able to grow correctly and not rot as they mature.

Water Requirements: Evenly moist, but do not overwater

Soil pH: 6.5

Best Varieties: Danvers, Little Finger (can be grown in deep containers)

Best Companions: Beans, lettuces

Avoid Planting With: Herbs, tomatoes

Spacing: 6" to 8" apart in rows 12" apart

Planting Depth: ¼" deep, lightly covered, thin seedlings out into rows 8" t0 12" apart

Harvest: 25-40 days depending on variety, always harvest before tops go to seed

Special Considerations: Carrot greens can be eaten, too, so don't waste your tops! Make sure that you give your carrots enough space between plants to develop and get nutrients. Tightly-packed carrots can be stunted.

Celery

What to Know: Celery can be grown in two harvests, late spring, and early fall, as it tolerates cool temperatures and a bit of frost.

Water Requirements: soil should be kept evenly moist, never over-wet the soil

Soil pH: 6-7

Best Varieties: Conquistador, Alfina- look for "self-blanching" types to avoid having to mound up the soil around the roots as the celery grows

Best Companions: Peas, onions, beans

Avoid Planting With: Any nightshades- tomatoes, peppers, etc.

Spacing: Seeds should be directly sown in long rows 12" to 18" apart, thin seedlings

Planting Depth: ¼" deep, lightly covered

Harvest: 60-70 days for most varieties

Special Considerations: Homegrown celery is deeper in color than commercially-grown stalks because of mass cultivation practices. If you have a food dehydrator, you can chop and dry celery to use later in soups and stews or grind it up for celery salt. Celery stalks can also be frozen- just wrap them tightly in plastic or place them in freezer bags.

Chard

What to Know: Chard, also known as swiss chard or rainbow chard, for its bright-colored stems, is a terrific fast-growing, cool-season vegetable that brightens up any salad raw or soup or stew cooked. You can germinate the seeds and plant them indoors for a quicker harvest in the late spring or early summer.

Water Requirements: Soil should be kept evenly moist

Soil pH: 5.5-7

Best Varieties: Bright Lights, Peppermint

Best Companions: Lettuce, peas

Avoid Planting With: tomatoes, cucumbers

Spacing: plants 6" apart in rows 18" apart

Planting Depth: ½" inch, covered loosely and well-watered

Harvest: Cut as needed once mature; removing older leaves allows new leaves room to grow

Special Considerations: Chard is considered spent shortly before it goes to bolt, so make sure you finish harvesting when you see the center sprout- it will go bitter very quickly.

Garlic

What to Know: Garlic is an easy crop to grow, but it doesn't happen overnight. Garlic should be planted in the late fall for harvest the following summer, so keep that in mind as your garden winds down for the season- it's then time to plant garlic. Use bulb sets from seed suppliers, not grocery store garlic, for best results. Follow the supplier's instructions on pre-planting care as it is specific to variety.

Water Requirements: Garlic should be kept relatively dry when it's planted, but watering should ramp up during the spring, then taper off to every 3-5 days when you get near harvesting

Soil pH: 6-7

Best Varieties: Hardneck- German Red, Duganksi; softneck- Silverskin, California Early

Best Companions: Lettuce, tomatoes

Avoid Planting With: Beans, peas

Spacing: 2" to 4" apart in rows 12" to 16" apart

Planting Depth: Each clove should be at a depth of 2"-3" depending on how hard/soft your soil is

Harvest: Late spring to early summer, before the greens begin to flower

Special Considerations: Garlic can be stored for a very long time, as long as it is cleaned, dried, and cured properly. This depends on your variety, so follow the recommendations given on your bulb set packaging.

Green Beans (String Beans, Bush Beans, Pole Beans)

What to Know: Green beans are simple to grow and a garden favorite for many, but they come in other colors, too! Wax beans, purple kings, and Chinese red noodles offer similar flavors but an incredible variety of colors, so don't overlook their appeal.

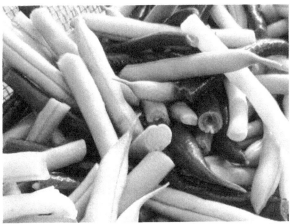

- beans don't always have to be green to be tasty -

Water Requirements: Beans are thirsty plants, so make sure you water them often and deeply

Soil pH: 6.5-7

Best Varieties: Blue Lake, Top Crop, Purple King, Goldmine

Best Companions: Squash, tomatoes

Avoid Planting With: Peas, lettuce

Spacing: Start indoors or out, plant seeds/seedlings 8" to 12" apart in rows 18" apart

Planting Depth: ½" deep, lightly covered, and evenly watered

Harvest: 65-75 days for most varieties; picking will encourage continual harvest

Special Considerations: Be sure to stake pole varieties early, so the vines have room to grow up and not out. This keeps the stems and leaves dry and happy. "Vertical" gardening also allows greater square footage on the ground for you to fit additional plants.

Kale

What to Know: Kale is very popular, and it can be easy to grow two harvests because it is cold-hardy enough to survive a light frost, but make sure to prep your soil before planting; it's a heavy feeding brassica, despite looking like a lettuce.

Water Requirements: Soil should be kept evenly moist

Soil pH: 6-7.5

Best Varieties: Winterbor, Red Russian

Best Companions: Beans, cucumbers

Avoid Planting With: Nightshades like tomatoes, peppers, and eggplants

Spacing: Plant seeds 6" to 8" apart in rows 12" to 16" apart, thin seedlings

Planting Depth: ¼" to ½", lightly covered and well-watered

Harvest: Kale is ready in about 60 days when the leaves are as big as your hand

Special Considerations: Kale, like most leafy vegetables, doesn't last long after harvesting. It should be kept cool and eaten or sold as soon as possible for the greatest freshness.

Head Lettuce

What to Know: Most lettuces require the same care but are harvested differently. Unlike loose or leaf lettuce, where you can pluck leaves as they grow, head lettuce should only be harvested once the plant is fully developed.

Water Requirements: soil should be evenly moist, never soggy

Soil pH: 5.5-7

Best Varieties: Great Lakes, Ithaca, Red Sails (for cooler zones)

Best Companions: Broccoli, carrots, cucumbers

Avoid Planting With: Peppers, peas

Spacing: Seeds should be in well-furrowed rows that are 12" apart

Planting Depth: No deeper than ¼", lightly covered; seeds need light to germinate

Harvest: 50-70 days depending on variety, when heads are full and solid and outer leaves begin to peel back

Special Considerations: Head lettuce does not keep long after harvest; heads should be cleaned and kept cool or refrigerated until consumption or sale.

Onions (Leeks, Scallions, etc.)

What to Know: Onions, leeks, and scallions (sometimes called spring onions) are all edible members of the amaryllis family known as alliums.

These growing tips apply to all these species, but the difference lies in when they are harvested and which part of the plant is consumed. Most true onion greens are bitter and inedible, and so we eat the bulbs. Scallions are much smaller and more tender, and the greens can be chopped for raw consumption and eating the tiny bulbs. Leeks are known for their thick, shiny tops and have a much earthier flavor. You can use both parts of the leek depending on what you are cooking.

Water Requirements: Alliums should be kept evenly moist but never wet; a deep watering once a week and a layer of mulch works well to maintain proper moisture levels and protect against weeds

Soil pH: 6.5-7

Best Varieties: Depends on species and variety

Best Companions: cucumber, lettuce, tomatoes

Avoid Planting With: beans, peas

Spacing: Alliums should be grown from sets (like garlic), 6" apart in rows 12" apart

Planting Depth: follow supplier directions for each variety

Harvest: for onions, when the tops have gone brown and wilted; for leeks, when the stalks are shiny, curved, and just begun to yellow at the edges; for scallions, just before the tops begin to flower; do not let alliums go to flower, they will be bitter

Special Considerations: Leeks and scallions should be consumed/processed/sold while fresh; onions can be cured and stored in cool, dry locations, hung in onion bags or open wooden crates.

Parsnips

What to Know: Parsnips are a flavorful root vegetable that can be grown in a season, or overwintered, as they are technically biennials. Parsnips are sativas, which means they share the same plant family as lettuces, but the greens should not be eaten- they can have mild-to-moderate toxicity.

Water Requirements: Like all root crops, parsnips need to be in well-drained soil, kept evenly moist but never swampy or soggy

Soil pH: 5.5-7

Best Varieties: Avonresister, Gladiator

Best Companions: Cucumber, beans

Avoid Planting With: Tomatoes, peppers, lettuces

Spacing: Seeds should be sown in well-furrowed, loosened rows 12" apart, spread seeds down the furrows, and thin seedlings to 4" to 6" apart

Planting Depth: ½" deep, lightly covered and well-watered

Harvest: For fall harvest, dig up your parsnips when the greens begin to flower. For spring harvest, cut the greens down the ground and cover the area with a thick layer of mulch. Dig the parsnips after the last spring frost.

Special Considerations: Parsnips left to overwinter will be sweeter than parsnips that are harvested in the fall. Make sure you remove the tops before they flower/go to seed, or they will self-sow and create an unwanted cycle where new seedlings and maturing roots have to compete for nutrients.

Peas

What to Know: Peas are quick-growing, can be planted early and often, and sport fragrant, delicate flowers that add beauty and draw pollinators to your garden. Peas are also legumes, which means they add much-needed nitrogen back into the soil as they grow.

Water Requirements: Pea plants like evenly moist, well-drained soil

Soil pH: 6-7

Best Varieties: Super Sugar Snap, Green Arrow, Snowbird

Best Companions: Squash, cucumbers

Avoid Planting With: Beans, tomatoes

Spacing: Direct sow seeds or start indoors; seedlings should be 12" to 18" apart in rows 12" inches apart; stake vines early to maximize plant health and garden space

Planting Depth: ½", covered and watered

Harvest: Begin harvesting pods when you can just see the peas bulging, 55-70 days for most varieties. The earlier you pick them, the sweeter they will be. If you want to dry the peas, you can let them mature and grow larger on the vine before harvesting. Most pea varieties will offer a continuous harvest if you pick them frequently. If you live somewhere with a long growing season, you can also plant new seedlings every three weeks or do a spring and fall planting to maximize your harvest.

Special Considerations: Peas are one of those versatile vegetables that can be eaten whole or shelled, cooked or raw; they can also be dried, canned, and frozen for later consumption. Think about what you want your end product to be when choosing varieties.

Potatoes

What to Know: Potatoes are one of the world's most abundant crops, and they can be planted early in the season. There is a lot of folklore surrounding the planting date of potatoes- from sowing after the full moon in March, or on St. Patrick and St. Gertrude's Day (March 17), to as soon as the first dandelions flower. In other words, mid-March is the best time to put your seed potatoes in the ground, but the stories are a bit of a fun touch.

Water Requirements: Potatoes should be kept evenly moist but never too soggy; make sure your soil is well-drained to avoid rot, hilling the soil up around the roots to prevent exposure helps with drainage AND protects the flesh of the tubers from going green, which makes them taste bitter and can cause nausea in some people

Soil pH: 5.5-6.5

Best Varieties: Yukon Gold, Irish Cobbler are great "beginner" potatoes; consider branching out into other colors and heirloom varieties once you've developed your gardening skills

Best Companions: Lettuce, beans, peas

Avoid Planting With: Tomatoes, peppers, eggplant (other nightshades), corn

Spacing: Seed potatoes should be planted 18" to 24" inches apart, in rows 18" to 24" inches apart

Planting Depth: follow supplier instructions based on variety

Harvest: Depends on variety, but the general rule is that potatoes are ready to be dug when the topside foliage dies back

Special Considerations: Potatoes can be cured and put into dry storage, but be sure to eat or process any that have damaged skin right away. Never put any bruised potatoes into long-term storage, and don't store them next to apples. Apples emit ethylene, which can hasten your potatoes to over-ripen.

Radishes

What to Know: Radishes are a popular root crop that can be grown in almost any soil due to their compact size. Check out varieties for their "bite" before deciding- some are decidedly sweeter than others, and some can be quite sharp and spicy. They can be harvested in less than a month so that you can try out a few different types during a single growing season.

Water Requirements: Like all root crops, radishes like to be evenly moist but not swampy

Soil pH: 6.5-7

Best Varieties: Daikon, Burpee White, French Breakfast

Best Companions: Lettuce, peas

Avoid Planting With: Beans, tomatoes

Spacing: Plant seeds in long furrows 8"-12" apart and thin seedlings to 2" to 4" apart to avoid crowding

Planting Depth: ½" to 1" deep, loosely covered and well-watered

Harvest: Every 3 to 4 weeks during the growing season, if you plant continuously

Special Considerations: Radishes are very nearly a perfect vegetable- they grow quickly, they are frost-hardy, and they keep well after harvesting. The only thing to keep in mind about radishes is that they mustn't get over-wet, so watering them deeply once a week or so and then keeping them covered in mulch is a great way to nurture the small roots without letting them get or stay too soggy.

Spinach

What to Know: Spinach is a widely used leafy green that is nutrient-dense, as well as supremely cold-hardy. You can grow spinach early and late in the season to get two harvests.

Water Requirements: Spinach is thirsty, so water well and often, but don't let the roots get too swampy

Soil pH: 6.5-7

Best Varieties: Tyee, Giant Noble

Best Companions: Beans, cauliflower, broccoli

Avoid Planting With: Tomatoes, peppers

Spacing: Seeds should be planted in rows 12" to 18" apart, thin seedlings to 8" to 10" apart

Planting Depth: ½" to 1", lightly covered and well-watered

Harvest: Spinach can be harvested by taking the outer leaves or by cutting the whole plant; avoid waiting until leaves are too large, or it will be bitter

Special Considerations: Spinach must be picked before it begins to flower, or the flavor will be ruined. Spinach doesn't keep very long, so it must be used or sold within a week at most for the best quality.

Turnips

What to Know: These popular root vegetables can be enjoyed for both their greens and the turnips themselves, and they mature quickly, allowing you to plant in both the spring and the late summer for two harvests. Fall turnips are generally sweeter and mealier than spring turnips, especially if you wait until after the first frost to harvest them.

Water Requirements: Like all root vegetables, keep the soil evenly moist but not soggy

Soil pH: 6-7

Best Varieties: Just Right, Golden Globe

Best Companions: Beans, broccoli

Avoid Planting With: Tomatoes, corn

Spacing: Seeds should be sown in rows 12" to 18" apart, thin seedlings to 4" to 6" apart when the greens are 4" tall

Planting Depth: ½", loosely covered

Harvest: Greens can be clipped after 45 days; mature turnips can be dug in 60-70 days

Special Considerations: Turnips can be kept in dry storage for up to four months, but if you refrigerate them, they will likely only last for no more than two weeks. Plan accordingly for your crop.

Watermelon

What to Know: Watermelon is clearly not a vegetable, but it's an exceptional companion plant, draws pollinators, and frankly, who doesn't love watermelon? Melons come in all shapes and sizes and can be grown vertically to save space. Some compact varieties do well in large containers, as well.

Water Requirements: Melons need a lot of water because they are fruit with a high moisture content; be sure your soil is well drained to avoid root-rot

Soil pH: 6-7

Best Varieties: Sugar Baby, Sugar Daddy, Sweet Beauty

Best Companions: Tomatoes, broccoli, peas

Avoid Planting With: Beans, cucumbers

Spacing: Seeds/seedlings should be 12" to 18" apart in rows 18" apart, hill the soil around the germinating seeds

Planting Depth: No deeper than 1"

Harvest: Melons are considered ripe when they are heavy on the vine but make a hollow sound when thumped; this lets you know the insides are water-dense, meaning juicy fruit

Special Considerations: Once melons appear on the vines, you should stake them up or wind them over a trellis. Leaving melons lying on the damp ground invites pests and pathogens. Melons should be consumed or sold within two weeks of harvest.

Chapter 9: Planting Full Sunlight Vegetables

These are the vegetables that you'll want to plant in the sunniest spaces in your garden because they thrive on as much light as they can get. These are varieties that are either harvested or planted in the height of summer, and the long hot days and short cool nights are what affect the flavor and quality of the harvest.

Acorn Squash (Winter Squashes)

What to Know: Winter squashes, like acorn, butternut, pat-a-pan, and others, are the cold-weather cousins of the cucurbit family, which also includes cucumbers, some melons, and summer squashes, of course. These varieties have thick, hardened skin and can be prepared in a number of ways but are rarely eaten raw. They also keep longer than summer squashes.

Water Requirements: Squash has a high moisture content, so keep soil evenly moist

Soil pH: 6.5-7

Best Varieties: Tuffy (acorn), Butterscotch (butternut), Sugaretti (spaghetti)

Best Companions: Corn, beans, peas

Avoid Planting With: Tomatoes, eggplants, potatoes

Spacing: Seeds should be sown in rows 18" to 24" inches apart, thin to 12" to 18" inches apart, or place seedlings at this distance

Planting Depth: No more than 1" deep, lightly covered and well-watered

Harvest: For most varieties, 65-80 days, at or just after the first frost

Special Considerations: Winter squash can be cured and will last for a few months if stored in a cool, dry location. Any damaged fruit should be processed, consumed, or sold within two days of harvest.

Beans (Pod/Runner Beans)

What to Know: These beans are the ones you think of when you think of soups or ethnic cuisines like Mexican or Italian. We're talking about red beans, black beans, Yankee and navy beans, black-eyed peas, and other such legumes that can be shelled, dried, and used for a variety of culinary purposes. These beans, when dried, also make terrific craft supplies for gardeners with artsy tendencies or crafty kids. They are the essential ingredient for any coffee-can percussion instrument and make colorful mosaics projects.

Water Requirements: These beans can be thirsty; water deeply and often, especially early in the season

Soil pH: 6.5-7

Best Varieties: Dragon's Tongue, Dixie Butterpea, Black-eyed Beauty

Best Companions: Squash, corn, cucumbers

Avoid Planting With: Tomatoes, peppers

Spacing: Seeds should be thinned, or seedlings placed 12" to 18" apart in rows 18" to 24" inches apart

Planting Depth: ½", lightly covered and well-watered

Harvest: For most varieties, 65-75 days; can continuously harvest with regular picking

Special Considerations: Beans are easy to dry for future use. Just wash and pat them dry, and lay them out on a flat surface where they can be undisturbed. When the pods are dry and brittle, snap them open and store the beans in an airtight container or in a sealed freezer bag in the freezer until ready to use. Soak to wash and rehydrate.

Cauliflower

What to Know: Cauliflower is a garden staple and is considered one of the most nutritious, versatile vegetables you can grow. Although we're used to seeing white cauliflower, it comes in a variety of colors and grows quickly enough to plant two harvests per season. Cauliflower tolerates frost well, meaning you can plant it early in the spring and late in the summer to maximize production.

Water Requirements: Keep soil evenly moist but not soggy; avoid watering the growing heads

Soil pH: 6-7

Best Varieties: Snowball, Flamestar (yellow/orange), Graffiti (purple)

Best Companions: Broccoli, Brussels sprouts, cucumbers

Avoid Planting With: Tomatoes, eggplants

Spacing: Seeds should be sown in furrows set 18" apart, thin seedlings to every 12"

Planting Depth: No deeper than ½", lightly covered; water on the second day

Harvest: When heads are 6" to 8" across and firm; 65 days for most varieties

Special Considerations: Cauliflower is now used for so much more than just a side dish. Consider adding recipes for cauliflower dishes as a value-added product, so consumers become interested in trying new tastes and varieties.

Corn

What to Know: Corn is one of the only things you'll grow in your vegetable garden that is wind-pollinated rather than relying on insects and birds. If you want to grow corn, you need to grow enough of it that it can be pollinated, and you have to have it in the open enough location that it can catch the breeze. Corn is a heavy feeder, so prep your soil with lots of compost and side-dress at least once during the season. Plant corn early in the season, about two weeks after the last frost, so it has time to grow, flower, and mature by mid- to late summer.

Water Requirements: Corn is THIRSTY- water it often, at the roots, but don't let it get soggy; corn has a shallow taproot and exposed supporting rootlets; target your water to the center of the root

Soil pH: 6.5-7

Best Varieties: Silver Queen, Sweet Sunshine, Painted Mountain (ornamental)

Best Companions: Squash, cucumbers, beans, peas

Avoid Planting With: Tomatoes, peppers, eggplants

Spacing: Place seeds in well-turned soil, thin seedlings to 12" apart

Planting Depth: 1½" to 2" deep, well-covered, and watered

Harvest: When ears are +/-8" long, and the cornsilk is peeking from the husk

Special Considerations: Sweet corn begins to lose its sweetness once it is picked, so be sure to eat, process, or sell it as fresh as possible for the best flavor. Corn can be boiled, roasted, and even grilled to make things interesting, or you can strip the kernels to can or blanch and freeze to enjoy later.

Cucumbers

What to Know: Cucumbers have long been a staple in home gardens and are popular for their crisp taste and refreshing crunch. They are a quintessential summer vegetable, and they can be enjoyed long after the harvest as pickles. There is a multitude of varieties, including large vining plants and "bush" sizes, which grow well in containers and small spaces.

Slicing Cucumbers

VS

Pickling Cucumbers

- cucumbers come in many sizes and varieties for snacking and preserving -

Water Requirements: Cucumbers may be the thirstiest plant in the garden; water deeply and often

Soil pH: 6-7

Best Varieties: Straight 8, McPick, Picklebush, Sassy

Best Companions: Beans, peas, corn

Avoid Planting With: Tomatoes, squash

Spacing: Seeds/seedlings should be 12" to 18" apart in rows 12" apart

Planting Depth: ¼" to ½" inch, lightly covered and well-watered

Harvest: When the blossom falls off the fruit; 60-70 days for most varieties; avoid letting them get too big, or they will be pithy and bitter

Special Considerations: Cucumbers don't last long off the vine, so you should plan to consume, sell, or process them into pickles within a few days of harvesting. They love the sun, and vining cultivars should be given vertical space to ensure the whole plant gets enough sun. This also makes more space in the garden and keeps the tender fruits off the ground as they grow.

Eggplant

What to Know: Eggplant is in the same family as tomatoes, peppers, and potatoes, which are commonly referred to as nightshades. While the purple eggplant is the most recognizable, they also come in white and green varieties. Eggplant is a heavy feeder, so plan on side-dressing during the season.

Water Requirements: Keep soil evenly moist but never soggy

Soil pH: 6-7

Best Varieties: Black Beauty, Dusky, Casper (white), Kermit (green)

Best Companions: Onions, carrots, peas

Avoid Planting With: Other nightshades

Spacing: Seeds/seedlings should be 12" to 18" apart in rows 18" inches apart

Planting Depth: No more than ½", cover well and water deeply

Harvest: 60-70 days for most varieties; pluck when the fruit is full but not heavy, which indicates seediness

Special Considerations: Eggplant is one of those vegetables that people seem to either love or hate. Gauge your market if you want to grow eggplant for sale; you don't want to end up with too many unwanted fruits on your hands.

Okra

What to Know: Okra is a bit of a specialty vegetable, but it is very popular in the southern United States, where it's used in soups, stews, and gumbos, or sliced, breaded, and fried. It thrives in hot weather, so plan your planting date accordingly so it can mature during the hottest, steamiest part of your summer. Okra flowers are also beautiful and fragrant, adding to the appeal of your garden and drawing pollinators.

Water Requirements: Okra is thirsty, so water well and often

Soil pH: 6-7

Best Varieties: Annie Oakley II, Cajun Delight

Best Companions: Peas, carrots, beans

Avoid Planting With: Tomatoes, onions

Spacing: Seeds/Seedlings should be 18" to 24" apart, in rows 24" apart

Planting Depth: ½", lightly covered and well-watered

Harvest: 55-65 days for most varieties, when pods are 2"-3" long; trim away lower leaves to extend the growing season; wear sturdy gloves as okra plants have tiny, prickly spines along their stems

Special Considerations: Okra is a terrific source of vitamins and is low in calories, so it makes a terrific addition to heart-healthy diets. If you don't want to use your okra right away, it can be pickled, sliced, and dehydrated, or blanched and frozen. If you don't have a lot of space and want to grow okra, you can get compact varieties that do well in large pots; just make sure they are well-drained so the roots have room to spread out without getting soggy.

Peppers

What to Know: Peppers come in a ton of varieties, from the sweet bell pepper to the hottest chilies. The difference between the types of peppers is the amount of capsaicin that they contain, which is what gives peppers their signature heat. They all require tons of sunshine and warm weather to grow and mature properly, so starting seeds indoors or buying seedlings is a great way to ensure that your pepper plants will get off to a good start before even getting into the garden soil. Plan to side-dress during the season, as peppers are very heavy feeders.

Water Requirements: Peppers are nightshades, so water often and deeply

Soil pH: 6-7

Best Varieties: Lady Bell, Bellboy, Flamethrower, Rainbow Chili

Best Companions: Peas, lettuce

Avoid Planting With: Broccoli, beans

Spacing: Seedlings should be no closer than 18" apart in rows 12" to 18" apart

Planting Depth: Seeds should be started indoors, ½" deep in seedling cells, lightly covered and well-watered

Harvest: Most varieties begin maturing after 60 days, some as long as 90; follow supplier instructions based on variety

Special Considerations: Peppers of different colors don't come from different plants! A green bell pepper is one that was picked immediately upon maturity- a few more days on the vine, and it will begin to change from green through yellow, orange, and finally, red. You can harvest based on personal preference. Due to their need for a long growing season, be sure to plant your pepper seedlings as soon as you can for your area, or you won't have any ready for the end of summer, and the plants are not frost-hardy.

Pumpkins

What to Know: Pumpkins are winter squash, which means they need lots of space to spread their vines. They're also in the same family with cucumbers and melons, so they must be well-watered, or the flesh will end up dry and mealy. With one of the longest growing seasons of any common garden veggie, it's important to get your pumpkin seeds or seedlings in the ground as soon as the last threat of frost is gone in the spring, especially if you want to have small pumpkins for early fall eating and larger pumpkins for late fall festivities.

Water Requirements: Water well and often, but don't let the roots get soggy; soil should be well-drained

Soil pH: 6-7

Best Varieties: Rouge vif d'etampes, Jack Be Little, Little Giant, Sugar Treat (pie pumpkin)

Best Companions: Peas, beans

119

Avoid Planting With: Broccoli, cauliflower

Spacing: Seeds/seedlings should be no less than 18" apart; 24" is better; plant in hills of mounded-up soil to give roots an extra early advantage

Planting Depth: ½" deep, lightly covered and well-watered

Harvest: 75-100 days for most varieties; mature pumpkins have a hollow sound when thumped and should feel "heavy for their size"

Special Considerations: Pumpkins need a lot of space to spread their vines, but miniature varieties can be grown vertically on trellises. You can also plant them on the margins of your gardens so they can spread out without smothering any other plants. Consider planting vining peas or beans that you can stake up in the center of your pumpkin patch so that the legumes can help nourish the soil as the heavy-feeding pumpkins deplete it.

Sweet Potatoes

What to Know: Sweet potatoes aren't potatoes, nor are they yams. Both of these are common misconceptions about this nutritious root vegetable that grows very well in warmer climates. They are actually in the morning glory family, and the vines and leaves make a terrific ornamental ground cover, as well. They should only be planted when the weather leaves no threat of frost, and they need a lot of space to grow.

Water Requirements: Soil should be kept evenly moist but never soggy

Soil pH: 6.5-7

Best Varieties: Beauregard, Jewel, Vardaman

Best Companions: Peas, lettuce

Avoid Planting With: Tomatoes and other nightshades

Spacing: Seedlings should be placed no closer than 18" apart, in hills or mounds to encourage root growth

Planting Depth: According to variety; follow supplier recommendations

Harvest: When leaves have yellowed on the vine, 90-100 days for most varieties

Special Considerations: Sweet potatoes can be left out to cure in a warm spot for 10-14 days, then packed in newspaper and stored in a cool, dry location. They will keep for up to four months in dry storage. Any damaged vegetables should be processed into a puree or eaten within a few days.

Tomatillos

What to Know: Tomatillos are fun to grow because they have such an interesting foliage, and the fruit has built-in packaging of sorts. Tomatillos must be planted in pairs or bunches, as they cannot be pollinated from the same plant. They have a sweet, spicy taste that works well in salads, salsas, and many Spanish-style cuisines, not to mention it's just fun to peel the papery skins off of them.

- tomatillos are a fun vegetable that you can use in a variety of dishes for their tangy, slightly spicy flavor -

Water Requirements: Tomatillos are thirsty; water them as you would a tomato plant

Soil pH: 5.5-7

Best Varieties: Toma Verde, Verde Puebla, Purple Di Mipla

Best Companions: Beans, peas, squash

Avoid Planting With: Tomatoes, peppers

Spacing: Seeds/seedlings should be a minimum of 12" apart in rows 18" apart

Planting Depth: 1/4", lightly covered; water the next day

Harvest: 70-80 days for most varieties; don't wait until the papery outer skin splits or the fruit will be overripe

Special Considerations: Tomatillos can be super productive, but remember they must be planted with at least two plants to furnish you with any fruit. They are hardy plants, but the fruits are tender and spoil quickly, so consume, sell, or process them within a few days of harvest. Just a few plants can keep you in canned salsa for months when grown properly. Plan to side-dress these hungry vegetables about half-way through the season for best results.

Vine Tomatoes

What to Know: These tomatoes are the larger, more expansive cousins of the bush varieties, but you can still grow them in large containers if you'd like. Vining tomatoes need a lot of support as they grow, so make sure you've got sturdy stakes or tomato cages at the ready before the plants get heavy with fruit. Plan on side-dressing your hungry tomatoes during the season; like all nightshades, they are heavy feeders and need a lot of nutrients and organic material to thrive. You can pinch off any suckers and trim leaves from the bottom of the plant to direct the plant's energy into growing tall and producing more fruit.

Water Requirements: Early and often; tomatoes have very high water content and need tons of water to grow healthy fruit

Soil pH: 5.5-7

Best Varieties: Cherokee Purple, Brandywine, Roma VF, Rutgers 250

Best Companions: Peas, beans, lettuce

Avoid Planting With: Other nightshades, squash

Spacing: Varies wildly by variety, follow supplier recommendations

Planting Depth: Generally ¼" to ½", follow supplier recommendations

Harvest: When fruit has reached its variety's intended size and color; green tomatoes can also be harvested for cooking

Special Considerations: There are thousands of tomato varieties available to the home and market gardener. You should consider attending a tomato-tasting event to choose the styles you want to produce and scope out your "competition" to see what they are and aren't growing. Remember that ripe tomatoes are fragile and should be sold, consumed, or processed as soon as possible to best taste and quality.

Zucchini (Summer Squashes)

What to Know: Squashes have been grown in North America for over 5,000 years, which means you have tons of knowledge to draw on when it comes to cultivating strong, productive squash plants. Summer squashes have a shorter growing season than their winter counterparts and don't cure and keep like their thick-skinned cousins. They are meant to be enjoyed when ripe.

Water Requirements: Squash roots should be kept evenly moist but never soggy

Soil pH: 5.5-7

Best Varieties: Silver Summer, Cashflow, Tigress

Best Companions: Corn, beans, peas

Avoid Planting With: Tomatoes and other nightshades

Spacing: Seedlings should never be closer than 12" apart

Planting Depth: ½", lightly covered and well-watered

Harvest: 55-70 days for most varieties; avoid 'monster zucchini' by harvesting when fruits are 12" to 15" long

Special Considerations: Squash plants can grow quite large, and their roots have a tendency to loosen as they grow. You can stake up or trim away large bottom leaves and hill up the soil over the roots to avoid them becoming dislodged from the ground. Summer squashes can be prepared in a multitude of dishes or shredded and used in baked goods like zucchini bread. Avoid planting too many summer squash plants because the adage about not being able to give zucchini away is based on some sad but hilariously true gardening lore.

Part 4:

Maintaining and Troubleshooting Your Garden

Chapter 10:
Nourishing Your Garden

B y now, you've got all the information you need to choose your garden's location and how to design and build the vegetable plot of your dreams. You have probably already decided what you want to grow, and now you know how to arrange your plants, so they are next to their best companions and have the proper amount of sun. Now let's take a deep dive into the process of nourishing your garden and giving it all the nutrients your plants need to stay strong and healthy from planting through harvest.

The Nutrients Your Plants Need

All plants require vital nutrients to grow and thrive. When gardeners talk about nutrients, they often refer to the big three- nitrogen, phosphorus, and potassium, or N, P, and K. These three elements are the macronutrients, meaning your garden needs these in the largest quantities. Without them, your plants cannot support their own biological processes. N, P, and K are the nutrients responsible for keeping your plant growing, green, flowering, and fruiting, so without them in the proper quantities, your garden won't be very successful. These nutrients are available to plants in abundance in healthy soil, but they can become depleted. That's why it's so crucial to have a soil test done and know your garden's baseline. That way, you can amend the soil to reach the correct levels and have happier plants.

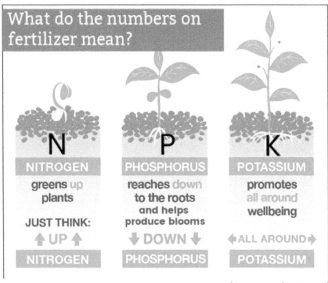

- an easy way to remember what the macronutrients do for your plants -

Your plants also need smaller quantities of other elements, known as micronutrients. This includes things like copper, calcium, boron, magnesium, and manganese, just to name a few. Your soil test report will also include levels of micronutrients. While amendments are rarely needed due to these elements' natural occurrence, you'll be able to see if adjustments do need to be made. Together with the macronutrients, micronutrients contribute to the overall health of your vegetable plants. A balance of nutrients will keep your garden happy and your veggies thriving.

Fertilizing Your Garden for the Season

When you're getting ready to plant your garden, soil health and nutrition is one of the things that should be at the forefront of your mind. If you want to keep the soil in top condition, you'll need to prep the soil before the growing season begins. You can do this by adding lots of organic material like some good compost and fertilizer. Working fertilizer into the soil before you plant means the soil will be well-stocked with nutrients before putting the first plant in the ground. A good time to fertilize is 10-14 days before you plant. You should apply your fertilizer to the bare soil, give it a good soaking to allow the fertilizer to leach into the ground, and then wait a few days before giving the soil a turn with a pitchfork or hand-tiller.

Fertilizers should always be used according to package instructions and to the letter. For most generic garden applications, you're going to want to

133

use a fertilizer that is labeled "10-10-10." Let's talk about what the numbers mean. On every fertilizer package, you'll see this series of three numbers, and they correspond with the macronutrients N, P, and K, in that order. What this means is each number tells you the ratio of nutrients in the fertilizer product. A 100-lb. bag of 10-10-10 fertilizer will have 10 lbs. of nitrogen (usually in the form of ammonium nitrate or NH_4NO_3), 10 lbs. of phosphorus (usually in the form of sodium phosphate), and 10 lbs of potassium (in the form of potash.) The rest of the package's volume will consist of fillers and binders and small amounts of other compounds that make the fertilizer more soluble. Fertilizer can be purchased in a variety of ratios, like 10-5-10, 5-5-5, etc. You get the idea. Most lawn fertilizers contain no phosphorus and have a zero in the middle. This is because many states ban the use of phosphorus on lawns because it leaches easily, and the run-off can damage the water table. We're telling you this so you don't think you can use your extra veggie fertilizer on your grass. Please don't!

Liquid vs. Solid Fertilizers

With so many fertilizers available on the market, how can you know what's best for you and your garden? You can choose from liquid or granulated fertilizers, organic options, spread-or-spray choices, and combination products; it can be difficult to decide which will fit your needs. The first thing to do is read the labels. If you're more comfortable with liquid products, check out the application instructions and see if it is ready-to-use or a concentrate. If it's a concentrate, how will you dilute and diffuse it? Some liquid fertilizers can be put in a hose sprayer attachment that mixes the water into the product before dispersing it. Some need to be mixed in a sprayer jug (these usually hold two gallons of liquid) and delivered manually.

- liquid fertilizers are usually diluted and sprayed manually -

Solid fertilizers come in granules and need to be broadcast over your soil. You can get a walk-behind spreader if your garden is large, or you can use a repurposed flour sifter if your garden is made up of small plots and raised beds. You should be mindful of the instructions when using solid fertilizers. Be sure you have the proper measurements of your garden, so you don't overfertilize. More is not always better, and too much fertilizer can lead to toxicity and harm your plants. If you have any concerns or questions, ask them before you apply your fertilizers. You can call your local Cooperative Extension or farm bureau for advice. These offices have staff and trained volunteers who can assist you in using fertilizers and other gardening questions.

The same rules apply for using liquid fertilizers. Always make sure you understand the dilution and application instructions before you begin spraying. Liquid fertilizers come in a couple of varieties. Whether you decide to use chemical or organic liquids, you still need to take care not to overfertilize. Most liquid fertilizers are in concentrated form, so take care to wear gloves and eye protection when you open the containers. No one wants a splash of liquified fish meal to the eye, trust us.

If we're being honest, we don't recommend combination products, at the very least for a brand new garden. Some of these products combine fertilizer and weed prevention or fertilizer and pesticide. Why isn't this a good thing? To begin with, you've got a brand new garden. You don't know what type of weeds or pests you might get. You might not have any! Then you've treated your soil with unnecessary chemicals, and that's never a good thing. We discourage the use of combination products because it's hard to tell if you're really using the proper amount, even following the package directions. The bottom line is, if you want your garden to function as a cohesive system, you have to treat every part separately to make sure it fits into the ecological flow.

Supplementing while Your Garden Grows

During the growing season, your soil will become depleted, especially if you have a lot of heavy feeders like tomatoes and other nightshades. The question becomes, can I fertilize again mid-season? The answer is yes! This is called side-dressing, and it's a bit more targeted than your pre-season preparatory fertilization. When you side-dress your garden, you choose to supplement the plants that need the most TLC during the season.

You can side-dress with a measured amount of granules or diluted liquids delivered directly to the soil at the base of your plants. Try not to let the fertilizer get anywhere that it can harm plants that don't need it- remember too much can cause some toxicity issues. Unlike when you fertilize before planting, you are going to side-dress AFTER watering the garden for the day. When you prep, you want the fertilizer to leach into the soil and spread out. When you side-dress, you want to give the fertilizer time to reach the roots of the plants you are treating. Let the fertilizer rest for a bit before you water again.

Another way to supplement your garden while it's growing is compost. Like we've said, you can never overdose on organic material. Compost is a terrific way to give your plants some love in the middle of the growing season, and making your own compost is easy and free, sans a little labor. Composting frightens some people who've never given it a try, but once you get started, it's fun, resourceful, and a great way to nourish your garden for minimal effort.

Let's talk for a moment about what compost even is. Compost is the end result of organic decomposition, and it's rich in nitrogen and carbon. Have you ever taken a walk in the woods and seen the soil underneath the leaf litter? If you close your eyes, you can probably even imagine the smell; it is rich and earthy, a little tangy, even. That dark soil under the leaf litter is actually a material known as humus. Not hummus- that's a tasty dip made from chickpeas. Humus. Humus is what you are trying to achieve in your compost heap. It's dark and crumbly and will make your garden even more amazing!

Compost can be made from many fibrous materials. Kitchen food scraps are a great go-to item to start your compost heap. Although meats and cheeses should never be composted because they cause odor, attract vermin, and don't break down well, you can compost almost anything else in your kitchen. Fruit and vegetable peels and trimmings, eggshells, bread products, used paper towels (yup!), coffee grinds, and tea bags are an excellent place to start. Get a small container you can keep under the sink to toss all your compostable waste. Other household items that can be composted are shredded newspaper, uncoated paper, and cardboard. Avoid putting any coated or glossy paper (like magazines or advertising inserts) into the compost. It can contain chemicals you don't want in your soil.

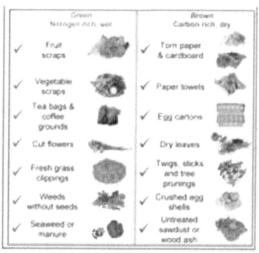

Green Nitrogen rich, wet		Brown Carbon rich, dry	
✓ Fruit scraps		✓ Torn paper & cardboard	
✓ Vegetable scraps		✓ Paper towels	
✓ Tea bags & coffee grounds		✓ Egg cartons	
✓ Cut flowers		✓ Dry leaves	
✓ Fresh grass clippings		✓ Twigs, sticks and tree prunings	
✓ Weeds without seeds		✓ Crushed egg shells	
✓ Seaweed or manure		✓ Untreated sawdust or wood ash	

- almost all organic material can find its way to your compost heap -

Outside, your regular yard work can contribute to the compost heap, too. Leaves, small twigs and branches, and grass clippings all break down and release beneficial nitrogen. A good thing to remember when putting things into the compost is that the larger they are, the longer it will take for them to break down. Leaves decompose faster when they're mulched, and twigs and other woody trimmings should be trimmed into short pieces. You want to do as much as you can to encourage decomposition so you can 'harvest' your compost in a shorter amount of time. Once you have a healthy, functional compost heap, it becomes self-renewing. It's just hard to be patient to get that first batch of rich, nutrient-loaded humus.

Now, to building and maintaining that compost heap. There are several different approaches to this, and the one you choose depends on how much compost you want to make, what amount of labor you can put into your compost, and how much time and resources you want to take building it. The most basic compost heap is just that- a heap. All you need to do is choose a location, mark it out with some bricks or pallets, and start a pile. If you're feeling fancy about it, you can get several cheap metal fenceposts, pound them into the ground and slide reclaimed wood pallets over them, essentially making a large wooden "crate" to contain your pile. You can achieve the same effect with posts and a length of chicken wire. The more airflow you can get to your compost heap, the faster it will decompose, and you'll avoid odors.

If you do build an open heap of some sort, you can cover it with a tarp to keep in the heat of the biological processes of decomposition. When you maintain a closed environment for your compost, it's called hot composting. This isn't necessary, per se, for a small home gardener or market gardener, but lots of bigger farms and commercial producers use this method. That's because they are often composting something you likely don't have at your disposal, and that's livestock manure. Hot composting is the preferred method of breaking down animal waste at large agricultural operations.

To maintain and grow an open compost heap, you'll want to add material to it in layers continuously. If you dump out your kitchen scraps, cover them with leaf litter, and then use a pitchfork to turn the pile so the new stuff gets to the bottom and the old stuff comes up to the surface. Then take your hose and give the whole thing a good soaking. Moisture will help the decomposition process along and keep the mess in check. You don't want it getting dried out and dusty, lest it blows away! Once your compost pile starts sustaining itself, you'll have plenty of material to enrich your garden.

Some people like to keep their compost a little more contained, and that's what self-contained compost turners are for. They take a lot of the muss and fuss out of a compost heap. These rotating barrels are great for people who don't have a large garden or ample space for an open compost pile. You can find them at a variety of price points from most garden suppliers, and they consist of a drum mounted to a frame so that the drum can spin freely- like a piece of meat on a spit. If you're handy, you can make one yourself; there are tons of plans available on the internet, along with instructional videos. To make compost in a turner, you just pop open the door in the side of the barrel, put your material in and wet it down. Now give it a turn every time you add new material. As it breaks down, it will sift through a screen mounted inside the barrel. Pop open the other door and catch your humus in a bucket or wheelbarrow. Simple!

Now that we've talked about all the ways you can nourish your soil and feed your plants, it's time to talk about watering. Let's move on to the next chapter and get soaked!

Chapter 11:
Watering Your Garden

Earlier, we touched upon the importance of watering your plants to maintain their maximum health. Plants need water for many of the same reasons people do- to help move nutrients through the circulatory system and to hold the structure of cell walls (which in turn helps plants stand up straight and strong). We can't impress upon you enough the power of water to perk up even the saddest plant. Let's talk about watering techniques and systems, shall we?

How Often Should You Water?

Have you ever heard the phrase, "if you're thirsty, you're already dehydrated?" The same is true for your garden. If the soil looks dry, you're not watering enough. To answer the question at hand, you should water your garden often enough so that the soil never dries out. How often that is depends on a lot of factors. Do you live somewhere with high rainfall totals? Then you'll need to water less frequently. If you live in a drought-prone area, you will want to water at least once a day. It's also so crucial to have healthy, well-drained soil. When your soil is dry, compacted, or otherwise in need of TLC, it won't retain water very well.

Healthy soil has a good amount of what's known as pore space. This space between particles is what allows the soil to retain water naturally. When your soil has good pore space, those spaces fill up with water, and then the plants can use it as needed. There are three main classifications of soil particles, and they are based on size and texture. Sandy soil has the largest particles. They cannot sit very close together, and therefore, sand has great pore space. Unfortunately, sand by itself doesn't lend itself to being very fertile. It drains too quickly and erodes easily. The next type of soil particle is called silt. Silt is finer than sand and has less pore space. Silt is more fertile and retains more moisture. The third and smallest particle is clay. Clay can be packed very tightly and, by itself, is not the ideal garden soil. Water cannot penetrate clay soils and will run off and cause more harm than good. You want to have a mixture of the three to have the "perfect soil," and this mixture is broadly called loam. The best ratio for loam is 40% sand, 40% silt, and 20% clay.

What does all this soil talk have to do with watering? Your garden is an ecosystem, and all the parts have to work properly, or you'll have disfunction. If you built your garden in raised beds and imported the soil, you don't have to worry much about it. But if you're working in native soil, and you find that you're having water issues, it might not be how often you are watering, but the soil itself. You can amend your soil by giving it more texture to retain more water or drain better, depending on which direction you need to go. Heavy clay soils can benefit from having some sand mixed in to increase pore space and improve drainage. Conversely, sandy soil will be healthier with some smaller particles incorporated into it.

The point is that the quality and texture of your soil affect how often you need to water. Water retention is a vital component of the overall health of your garden. It can be helpful to observe what happens when you water your garden and see if there are any drainage issues. As a general rule, your garden needs and should get an inch of water a week. If your soil isn't retaining water, you're wasting your efforts. Make sure that the water is penetrating the soil and is draining properly. It will save you time, water, and labor in the long run. Another good trick is to keep a rain gauge somewhere in your garden. It will help you to know how much watering Mother Nature has taken care of for you.

Mulching your garden is another way to help your soil retain moisture. When most people think about mulch, they think of wood chips, but that's not always the best idea for a vegetable garden. Wood chips don't always break down very quickly, and some woods can leach tannins into your soil which can change the acidity. You can use things like grass clippings, straw, garden fabric, or plastic sheeting to help your soil retain moisture and heat, with the added bonus of weed suppression. Explore your options to decide what mulching method is best for your garden layout.

This is where we're going to sneak in a little note about weeding. DO IT. That is all. Don't make your plants compete for water and nutrients from plants that don't even belong in your garden.

Irrigation vs. Watering by Hand

Another age-old question when it comes to watering is, "how should I water?" This, again, is dependent on a lot of factors. Your available time, equipment, and resources will dictate what works best for you, as well as your physical capabilities and the size of your garden. Some people like to water by hand. It can be peaceful to spend some time in the garden every morning and gives you time to check out your plants up close. If you water by hand, be sure you're actually watering the soil and not just misting the plants. They take up water from the roots, not in through the leaves. Wet plants can also get sunscald, not to mention the dampness can invite pests and pathogens. This goes for tiny gardens that you water with a can or more extensive gardens for which you're using a hose.

If you're interested in installing an irrigation system, there are two routes you can take- drip irrigation and soaker hoses. These systems are similar in form and function but have a couple of key differences. Drip irrigation is much more targeted than soaker hoses. Drip irrigation consists of a series of thin tubes that you run through the garden. The tubing has small holes in it at set intervals, and the end of the tubing is coupled to your water source. When it's turned on, the water flows through the system and delivers water directly to the roots of the plants that are near the holes.

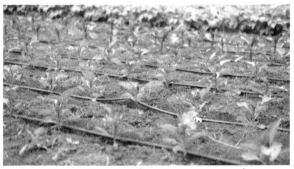

- drip irrigation takes a targeted approach to watering your garden -

Soaker hoses also couple to your water source, but these hoses are much thicker in diameter, like a regular hose. They are made of a semi-permeable material that allows the water to seep through and into the soil. Soaker hoses are a good option for large gardens and in drought-prone areas. Both drip irrigation systems and soaker hoses can be set on a timer to make sure they turn on and off at the proper times each day. It's a great way to be a hands-off waterer, but you'll still need to go into the garden each day and take stock of how things are going. Irrigation is not a substitute for attention.

Both drip irrigation systems and soaker hoses can be purchased relatively inexpensively and come in pre-fabricated kits that fit your needs for length and can be assembled with ease and without breaking the bank. One last note about watering- don't use a sprinkler in your vegetable garden. They don't deliver water directly to the roots and just end up making a muddy mess. Better to put them on the lawn and let the kids play.

Chapter 12:
Harvesting Your Garden

Once you've grown an amazing garden, you have to harvest it, or why bother? Harvesting is one of the best parts of growing your own vegetables. There is something magical about snacking on a fresh tomato straight from the plant while you're piling peas into a harvest basket. There are certain tricks to harvesting that you should know, though, so let's go over some techniques.

The first tip applies to every plant in your vegetable garden, and that's to harvest in the morning, before you water. You want to remove your harvest from the plant in the coolest part of the day and before it gets wet. This gives the plants themselves all day to recover from the trauma of being cut or plucked before the evening dew and cooler temperatures set in. It's important to remember that plants are living organisms, and while they are not sentient, they do have bodily functions that require care. When a stem is broken or cut during harvesting, it can cause a shock to the circulatory system of the plant and cause an open wound. You want to make sure you're a gentle harvester and that you give your plants the best possible recovery.

- good harvest techniques are important for all your vegetables-

When you harvest, it's crucial that you cause minimal damage to the plants. You can use a sharp pair of garden shears to cleanly cut away mature squashes and cucumbers, leaving a 1-2" stem on the vegetables. When you reap legumes, grasp them firmly near the top, at the stem, and give a quick tug or twist to get the whole vegetable from the vine. Nightshades like tomatoes, peppers, and eggplants will tell you when they are ripe- they won't separate from the plant until they are ready. While it's okay to harvest green tomatoes, you want to leave peppers and eggplants until they peak. For other things like squashes, cucumbers, beans, and peas, it's actually a good idea to harvest them a day or two before they hit their peak- they will be sweeter and more tender. If you've ever seen a monster zucchini, they're technically overripe. The longer they are on the vine, the seedier they become, and they can be a little bitter.

Once you've harvested, you need to decide what you're going to do with your produce. If you're selling it, you want to make sure you give everything a good wash with cool (not cold) water and lay it out to dry. Then you can gently pack it up to go to market and store it in a cool, dry place until sale day. If you're picking for your own consumption, make sure you eat anything at peak, or that has any damage first, so you don't have any spoilage. You don't necessarily need to shove everything straight into the refrigerator. Fruits and veggies emit odorless ripening pheromones and need to be in open space to let those taper off. If you shove everything into a crisper drawer right away, they will continue to let off those hormones in an enclosed space and cause each other to overripen and accelerate breakdown. In other words, you can force your produce to go bad quicker, and no one wants that. Let your harvest breathe for a while before storing it.

If you've harvested vegetables that can be dry-stored, like potatoes, onions, garlic, winter squash, and others, you want to make sure that everything is completely dry before packing it away. Dry storage is a great way to make your garden last long into the off-season. Find a good place to "cure" your veggies for a week to ten days. This means laying them out in a cool, dry place to let them rest and breathe before packing. Bulbs like onions and garlic can be hung up in bunches to dry, and potatoes and squash can find a nice home on a utility table. Once the veggies are cured, you want to store them in crates or boxes that will allow some air circulation. Burlap or old newspapers make excellent layering materials that will absorb any extraneous moisture. Always dry-store your veggies someplace cool, dry, and dark, like the back of a closet or pantry.

- proper dry storage can preserve your harvest to enjoy the entire offseason -

If you plan on processing or preserving your harvest by either freezing or canning, make sure that you do so as soon as possible. Like driving a new car off the lot, depreciation on fresh produce begins the moment it is separated from the plant. You want to be certain that you're using your vegetables at the peak of freshness to maximize nutrient content and flavor. The same goes for anything you are going to be selling. Try to harvest as close to market day as you can, or if you're selling daily at a stand, be sure to replenish your stock often to offer customers the best value and quality.

Remember that harvesting is an ongoing task, and you want to check your plants every day for vegetables that are ready to be picked. Certain plants, like beans and tomatoes, will give you a steady flow of fruit as the harvest season wears on, while others, like carrots, should give you one good harvest at a time. Not all plants behave the same, but the more you garden, the more your intuition will increase about harvesting and knowing when a plant is spent. In the next chapter, we'll take a look at what needs to be done when your garden has given you all it can, and it's time to end the season.

Chapter 13:
Winterizing Your Garden

When you realize that the garden is winding down for the season, you need to take steps to protect and preserve your soil for the following year. We call this winterizing your garden, but you can affectionately call it "putting the garden to bed." Taking care of your garden in the fall will make things easier for you in the spring, and it starts with knowing how to handle all your spent plant material.

If the material is free of disease, it should be composted. This is an excellent way for last year's garden to fuel next year's garden in a continuous cycle. You want to make sure you pull roots, stems, leaves, and especially dropped fruit out of all your garden beds, break it all down, and let it rot on the compost heap for the winter. Since you'll also be adding leave litter and the last grass clippings of the year on the compost pile, autumn is the perfect time to build up a rich bank of nutrients for your garden in the spring.

Once your garden beds are all clear of the year's growth, you should work some already prepared compost into the soil and lay down a layer of straw. Mind you, not hay- what's the difference? Straw and hay are cut from the same plant, but hay contains seeds and straw does not; it is simply the mown and baled stems of the hay grass. You always want straw when doing any gardening projects, or else you may end up growing alfalfa where your tomatoes should be. You could also consider scattering some winter rye or clover seed and growing what's known as a cover crop. These crops put down roots to keep your soil active over the winter months and can be turned right into the garden to provide organic material in the spring.

- this garden uses straw to cover the beds for winter-

Whether you choose to use compost and straw or plant a cover crop, the idea is to protect your living soil in the off-season. You don't want to just leave your garden bare to the elements to erode or wash away in heavy winter precipitation. It's important to prevent anything that could damage your garden over the winter, especially if you want to monetize your harvests. Your garden is an important asset and needs lots of love.

The off-season is also when you should be planning next year's layout, and this gives us the perfect opportunity to talk about crop rotation since we've already talked about preventing erosion and runoff. If you are of a certain age, you'll have learned about the American Dust Bowl of the 1930s. This phenomenon lifted millions of tons of loose topsoil in the midwestern part of the United States and carried it off in massive, sky-darkening, at times even fatal, dust storms. What does this nearly-century-old disaster have to do with being a market gardener today?

We've mentioned a few times now that your garden is its own ecosystem. The soil is a key factor in that, and maintaining soil health is the most important thing you can do for your vegetables. One of the biggest contributors behind the Dust Bowl was monoculture; this is an agricultural term that refers to planting a single crop rather than having a biodiverse farm or garden. Fruit orchards are another enterprise that often falls prey to a monoculture, but the American Midwest was guilty of it to an extreme. Many of these farms grew shallow-rooted, disease-prone corn varieties, and those that didn't, grew cereal grains like wheat or barley.

Growing the same crop on the same land year after year has a couple of negative effects. We'll address the pest control aspect of monocultures in the next few chapters, but let's talk about the effects of a monoculture on the soil. In short, it's terrible. When you plant the same thing in the same space for consecutive seasons, the soil becomes depleted of all its nutrients. Some of our most common garden veggies are very heavy feeders, like tomatoes, peppers, corn, and some squashes and brassicas like broccoli and cauliflower. These plants strip the nitrogen and other macronutrients from your soil. That's why light feeders and legumes like beans and peas are so important to your garden's ecosystem. They put nitrogen back into the soil to replace what their heavy-feeding neighbors have taken out. When you rotate your crops every year, you give your soil a chance to recover from the takers and be nurtured by the givers.

The second major contributor to the Dust Bowl was erosion- the soil became so depleted of nutrients and organic material that it quite literally cracked, dried up, and turned to dust. Add in drought conditions, and it was a recipe for disaster. The ecosystem simply couldn't sustain itself anymore. Today, the soil in the Midwest is replenished and healing, and it's once again the breadbasket of

America. How was that achieved? To begin with, farmers began to realize that the scientists were right; their land was a living thing that needed to be better cared for. As commercial fertilizer formulas became more refined, farmers also started getting better equipment and education for using them, as well as the natural fertilizers, like manure and grass cutting, that they found around their farms.

They began to resurrect their soil and use crop rotation. As agricultural science grew as a separate, respectable discipline, new varieties of disease-resistance crops were developed. Farmers also started using cover crops and crop rotation, with the knowledge that keeping more organic material in the soil at all times would reduce the risk of mass erosion. Soybeans and peanuts began taking turns with corn and wheat, and farmers also soon learned that a third fallow year in the rotation would aid their land in healing even faster. Clover and hairy vetch became popular crops for those "non-harvest" years. These days, this can be referred to as "carbon farming" as farmers get rewarded for adding green spaces, amending the soil, and trapping carbon in the ground, where it doesn't pose a threat as it does as a greenhouse gas.

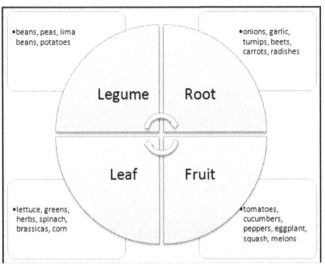

- crop rotation is the key to keeping your soil healthy year after year –

Okay, so, what does all of this have to do with your market garden? You may not have thousands of rolling acres of wheat fields, but you do need to protect your soil as an asset. Here's a handy little list for you- Leafy, Legume, Fruit, and Root. This is a terrific way to help you lay out your garden plan and perform proper crop rotation every year. So if you grow spinach, peas, cucumbers, and radishes- in that order from left to right- the next year, you'll bump everything over one spot- radishes, spinach, peas, and cucumbers. Do this every year, on top of your fertilizing and composting and winterizing, and you'll have continuously happy soil.

Chapter 14:
Troubleshooting Your Garden

When you're a gardener, you're so much more than just someone who puts seeds in the ground and watches them grow. You are a caretaker, a nurturer, a reader, writer, researcher, scientist, manual laborer, and perhaps, most importantly, a troubleshooter. Insects and diseases can invade even the best-kept gardens, and it is crucial to know how to find and solve any issues before they destroy your crops.

Although not everyone is expected to know everything about every potential problem that could strike, we like to focus on three big areas: Soil and water, pests, and pathogens. If you are diligent about preparing your soil and watering regularly, the first category should be an issue for you. When a garden is built well, even heavy rains and nasty summer storms don't have to be a major concern because you won't have to worry about soil erosion and run-off. Healthy soil retains just the right amount of pore space to take on the water it needs and allows the rest to drain away.

Healthy soil also has the right amount of nutrients to get your plants started, and adding compost and side-dressing with the proper fertilizer during the season will keep you in good shape. Correct winterization and sticking to a crop rotation plan is the last piece of the puzzle for maintaining good soil health. Not worrying about your soil and water is a huge burden off your mind, so plan and build a garden and a gardening routine that will help you in both the short and the long term.

How you build your garden and how you maintain it plays a huge role in having to deal with things in our next two categories, pests and pathogens. Moisture is both your best friend and your worst enemy. Too little, and your plants could wilt and die. Too much, and your roots could rot, and unfriendly microorganisms can move in and destroy your plants. That's why we always water the roots, not the leaves, and why there should be plenty of space between your plants for proper airflow. Unwanted pathogens like to grow in wet, dark spaces. Don't invite them in!

In the next chapter, we'll take an in-depth look at some common garden problems, how to identify them, and how to take action to mitigate the issues. No one wants to spend time, resources, and physical and emotional energy on planting a garden that fails! Let's go see how to avoid that with some vigilance and know-how.

Chapter 15:
Dealing with Pests and
Pathogens in Your Garden

Sadly, garden pests and pathogens are a part of life when you're undertaking any agricultural or horticultural pursuits. Making sure that your soil is as healthy as possible and having good watering routines and techniques go a long way towards eradicating any issues before they arise, but this often isn't enough. We've talked a few times already about thinking of your garden as an ecosystem, and that's the mindset that works best when dealing with unwanted visitors and microbes.

Integrated Pest Management

One popular way of handling pests and pathogens is an approach known as integrated pest management or IPM. IPM is a holistic view of a garden or farm as an interlaced ecological web, from the soil to the air to the plants and natural fauna. IPM seeks to answer the questions: What's going on in the garden? Why is this happening? What action can we take to adjust or re-balance the ecosystem? When you employ IPM, you are thinking about all the ways each component of your garden is dependent on the others to function properly.

Being observant and hands-on in your garden is the first step towards identifying and handling any issues. Spend time walking through your beds and checking your plants for any signs of disease or pests. There will always be tell-tale signs if you're in tune with what looks normal and what seems out of place. You may notice leaves changing colors when they shouldn't or insect activity that doesn't belong. Leaves and stems with physical damage and left-behind insect waste is a surefire way to know that somethings have been munching where they shouldn't be.

There are too many insect species and too many plant varieties to list here (and indeed, you can pick up entire books just about garden pest identification), but there are some common bugs you should familiarize yourself with. These include aphids, tomato hornworms (which affect all nightshades), thrips, cucumber beetles and squash vine borers, slugs and snails, caterpillars, Japanese and other Asian long-horned beetles, and mealybugs and grubs. And that's the shortlist! What's a gardener to do? Let's think about it from an IPM standpoint.

First, identify the insect. If you're unsure, take a photograph and hit the search engines. You can't fix a problem if you can't name it. If you're still stumped, grab a live (or dead) sample and contact your local farm bureau or Cooperative Extension. The trained staff and volunteers there can help you figure out what your insect is and how to stop it. Place the insect sample in a small airtight jar or seal it in an envelope. Try not to squish it too much, and never tape it to a piece of paper or a notecard. This destroys the shape and integrity of the insect for analysis.

Once you know what's eating your garden, you need to figure out why it's happening. Is your garden too wet, drawing moisture-loving insects? Maybe it's too dry. Maybe some bugs are just big jerks who love eating your peas. Once you've identified the pest and what drew it to your plants, you can formulate a plan to deal with it. IPM tells us that we need to adjust the ecosystem before we run straight to the harsh chemicals, especially since we're growing food. How can you eliminate insect pests from your garden without using extra-strength, industrial pesticides? It's actually easier than you think.

If you've got bugs eating your garden, you can up the game by inviting in things that eat the bugs. Put up birdhouses and bird feeders to draw in omnivorous songbirds to rid yourself of caterpillars and aphids. Put netting over the plants so the birds can eat the bugs without being able to eat the vegetables. Release ladybugs into your garden to eat aphids- they're like aphid vacuum cleaners, and it's also really cool to have tons of ladybugs on your plants. Don't disturb any spiders making webs, either- they are doing you a huge favor. You can also plant what's called a trap crop, where you set aside an area away from the main garden and toss in some leftover seeds to grow things that bugs like and draw them away from your real crop.

Sticky traps are another terrific option, as well as pheromone bag traps for beetles. Horticultural soaps are a watering additive that washes away pests and leaves the plant surfaces too slick for them to hold onto. These are non-toxic to food crops and are a useful tool in your IPM toolbox. For larger pests like caterpillars, manual removal is always an option if you've got time- just wear gloves. Some of the fuzzy and spiky caterpillar breeds can cause mild-to-moderate skin irritation, an example of natural defenses at their finest. Set out beer (yes, beer!) traps for slugs and snails. They can't resist the sugars and yeastiness, and they will fall in and drown. Gross, but highly effective, and a great way to get rid of the cheap swill left in the back of your fridge after your last party. If you don't have any, the least expensive 40-ouncer at your local bottle store will do the trick, and they're resealable. Only when all else has failed should you move onto harsh chemical pesticides. These are the last resort because they are often broad-spectrum, and you don't want to kill any beneficial insects or make any wildlife sick. You also don't want to pollute the water table when the pesticides work their way into the soil and get carried away by runoff. Always follow all packaging instructions, and don't be afraid to ask for help BEFORE applying if you don't understand the directions for application.

Speaking of wildlife, what should you do about your local furry woodland creatures? Fences and netting are your friends against deer and birds, for starters. Neither need to cost you much money, some simple metal pound-in posts can be found for cheap or free in many areas, and a roll of chicken wire is an inexpensive commodity. For rodents, sonic stakes are a great alternative to trapping and releasing. These stakes are usually solar-powered, just slide them into the ground on the perimeter of your garden, and they emit a high-pitched noise that humans can't hear, but drives rodents crazy. See you later, chipmunks. Be mindful of using these if you have dogs- you want to make sure you're getting ones that are marked that the frequency is safe for pets. No sense in making your canine companions unhappy!

Dealing with Disease

One of the other major concerns that plague gardeners are common plant pathogens, and here's where an ounce of prevention is worth a pound of cure. Proper plant spacing and good watering techniques are the best tools available to you to avoid disease. Again, your soil is also a factor in healthy plants. Healthy soil gives your plants a stronger immune system. You should also be choosing seed and seedling varieties that include disease-resistance in their descriptions. These actions all set up your garden for the best defenses against disease.

There are a handful of diseases you should familiarize yourself with, including blight, wilt, rust, mosaic viruses, powdery and downy mildews, end rot, and leaf spot and curl. These issues are all caused by microbes like bacteria, viruses, and fungi. As with pests, identification is the key to finding a solution, so use all your available resources. Not all of these pathogens will completely kill your plant, but you want to cut away and dispose of (NOT compost) any diseased material to try to save the plant. Cutting away the diseased material also tells your plant to redirect its energy towards growing and maturing healthy material, not to waste its resources on trying to fight the disease. You can also use antibiotic, antiviral, and antifungal applications as a last resort.

Sometimes, nutrient deficiencies and toxicity can mimic the effects of disease. Before you start pruning your plants down to nothing, ask: have I nourished this soil lately, or is it possible I over-fertilized? If your plants need more food, add compost. If it's possible that you applied too much fertilizer, give the plants extra water for a few days to try to flush their system. You might be able to salvage the situation. If not, lesson learned. Trash the plant and move on. The same goes for any plant that cannot recover from disease. You want to remove the infected plant(s) from the garden before any problems can spread.

Now that you know all the fundamentals of planning, building, planting, and maintaining your garden from seed through winterization, let's go back and revisit one of our major early topics-monetization. We'll finish up the book with a close-up look at growing your garden to grow your bank account, and then you'll have everything you need to get started! Shall we?

Part 5:

Monetizing Your Garden

Chapter 16:
Produce, Seeds, and
Seedlings- How to Sell Raw
Materials

When it comes to making money from your garden, we went over several ways to do so, including a vegetable stand, wholesale and retail agreements, and CSA subscriptions. But what do you REALLY need to do to monetize your vegetables? First, you need to focus on quality. There are a ton of small farms and market gardens pumping out tomatoes and zucchini, so you need to find something that's going to make you stand out. If you want to sell the same things as everyone else, then you need to be a standout at it to justify why someone should buy your product over someone else's.

The flip side of that coin is to specialize in something that fills a gap or a need. Does no one sell really good Brussels sprouts in your area? Become the best darn sprout gardener in the county, and you'll have an instant business. This can be one instance where the old adage, "do one thing and do it right," can play directly to your advantage. Choosing a focus doesn't mean you have to abandon all other pursuits, but it gives you a chance to build up an area of expertise and a specialty that will give you a good reputation in the market gardening world.

If you are interested in selling seeds and seedlings, then you can direct your energies into producing high-quality supplies for other gardeners. For seeds, this means that you will want to learn as much as you can about heirloom varieties. You will also need packing and labeling supplies, which can be purchased inexpensively in bulk and/or printed at home. When you label seeds, try to include as much information as you would find on a commercial seed packet and price them accordingly. Your seeds are lovingly harvested by hand, cleaned, sorted, and packaged by yours truly, and you want to sell them at a cost that will make sure you get paid a return on your investment.

Seedlings are a great enterprise that can be added to your produce sales because you're already planting, so why not plant more? Even if you're not in a position to grow a large garden, investing in some extra planting supplies and some plant labels is a great way to make money from your efforts. There are a lot of people who want to start a garden but don't have the time, wherewithal, or resources to start their own seeds, and strong, healthy seedlings are always a popular product in the spring.

Another raw material that you can sell from your property is compost. If you start composting and find that you're really good at it, you'll soon be producing more than you can use in your own beds. Bag it up, label it, and take it to the farmer's market with you! Tell people they can fill up a bucket for $5 when they come to pick up their other products-because compost works great for houseplants, too.

When it comes to selling raw materials from your garden, you should always check with your local health department to see if there are any regulations on food sales that you need to be aware of. If you intend to monetize your garden beyond a little bit of spending money, and especially if you want to have a CSA-style or U-Pick operation, you should incorporate it as a business, register your business name, and get basic liability insurance. A garden business is a business just like any other, so you want to protect yourself, your income, your property, and your customers. Be smart about it! Getting yourself off on the right foot early in the game will save you grief and paperwork down the road as you potentially grow and expand your operation.

Chapter 17:
Value-Added Products and Services to Boost Your Sales

Selling your raw materials like produce, seeds, seedlings, and compost doesn't have to be the only way you make money from your market garden. Think about some farm stands and farmer's markets you may have visited in the past. What were some of the other items for sale there, other than produce or other raw materials? What other products do you think you could add to your enterprise to make a little more money and draw in new customers?

Consumers love extras, and if you can provide them, you'll open new doors for your burgeoning business to grow and expand. If you have cottage food laws in your area (and in the United States, that's everywhere but New Jersey), you can look into what types of prepared foods you can offer under local regulations. This could be baked goods like savory pies and quiches (bonus if you raise your own chickens for the eggs), fruit and vegetable bread, and fruit pies and other treats. Some areas allow the

177

sale of homemade jams, jellies, and other canned and preserved items, and you may even be able to sell frozen items like blanched fresh vegetables.

- pickled items are always a customer favorite VAP –

If you took a basic agricultural business course, you would learn that these are called value-added products, and every activity that you undertake is called an "enterprise." The goal of value-added products is to choose things that mesh with what you're already doing to maximize your profits. For example, if you are already growing cucumbers, you can also process those cucumbers into other things like fresh cucumber salads and canned pickles. If you grow zucchini and pumpkins, you can also sell zucchini bread and pumpkin pie. It's all about taking your current enterprises and brainstorming ways to make the most from your efforts.

- fresh breads are a popular value-added product-

Value-added products give you the opportunity to be creative. We haven't talked much about growing things other than vegetables, this being a vegetable gardening book and all, but adding flowers and herbs to your garden has a lot of benefits beyond beautifying your space and drawing pollinators. You can bundle herbs and vegetables with a cute recipe card into a fun VAP that people will love- for example, tomatoes and basil with a recipe for Caprese salad or pizza Margherita. You can sell cucumbers, dill, and onions with a pickle or a salad recipe. The possibilities are endless.

If you grow flowers, there are obvious value-added products like cut bouquets, but you can also go beyond that into pressed flower artwork and dried potpourris. If you have a U-Pick garden, offer flowers as well as vegetables to draw more customers. It's also a nice touch to add a single cut flower in a CSA box with a tag that details how to buy bouquets or save seeds and use them as a nice giveaway or calling card to bring in new business.

There are also ways for you to include value-added services in your market garden. If you've got the proper insurance to have visitors on your property, there are so many possibilities open to you. Agritourism is a booming industry. You can host children's groups and classes where you "tour" the garden and learn about growing food. Toss in a snack and a craft, and you've got an entire afternoon program that can be lucrative and fun. Invite adults to farm-to-table events where you talk about fresh produce and create a snack or meal that people can enjoy and then purchase the products to make themselves at home.

Think about seasonal events for holidays and other celebrations. If you can get people into your market garden, they will purchase items. It's human nature. Hold seed planting classes and cooking demonstrations. Use your creativity to draw people to your property, and the business will naturally come with it. There is almost no end to what you can do with some brainstorming and some inexpensive supplies. Partner with other local businesses, if you can, for mutually beneficial events. Paint and sip classes are super popular, or you could invite a local chef to come to do a meal or class using your fresh ingredients.

If your property isn't set up to accept visitors, and that's fine, there are other ways to add value to your enterprises. If it's feasible for you, offer delivery to your customers. Adding just a modest fee can add up as you add more clientele, and people always appreciate a personal touch. You should also connect with local non-profit organizations. Donating your excesses to a food pantry or soup kitchen builds up your community equity and will drive people to your business to purchase your products.

There are so many opportunities to grow your gardening business beyond your fresh vegetables. You just need to put your thinking cap on, observe the industry around your area, and find a gap that needs to be filled. From offering classes on- and off-site to creating fun cooking kits to offering delicious ready-to-eat goods, adding value to your market garden is just a brainstorming session away.

Chapter 18: Building and Maintaining Your Business Model

A business is nothing without customers, and a well-run business is sunk without good recordkeeping and monetary practices. If you want to star, maintain, and grow a gardening enterprise, you have to give as much care to your accounting and your clientele as you do the garden itself. This starts with you, and there are some basic things you should be doing to make sure your business runs smoothly.

The first thing you need to do, and this goes for any gardener, is to keep a garden log. You want to record your garden designs, the materials you used (should you ever need to replace a part or some hardware), the seeds and seedlings you planted, and when. You should also record any applications you made, like fertilizer or pesticides, any actions you took, like planting, weeding, composting, and harvesting, and any issues you encountered. This record will give you a complete story of your garden for the year and will help you make decisions moving forward. You can do this by hand, of course, in a binder or notebook (handy for keeping seed packets and plant tags) or with any number of software programs, like a spreadsheet or table or online applications. There are many free or low-cost subscription services you can use to create a garden log that works for your sensibilities.

Keeping accurate records not only shows you everything that's happened in your garden over the course of the growing season, but it also gives you everything you need to expand into a gardening business. You can notate your transactions, use them for tax reporting, and if you're interested in any certifications, like being an organic producer, the records will help you with your applications to any governing bodies. Integrating your records with bookkeeping software will give you a complete picture of your garden and your business. You can see which enterprises are working for you and decide what direction you need to move in to improve your results both in the garden and for your bottom line.

You also need to attract and keep customers, so set goals and create a business plan. You can find a lot of guidance on business plans floating around out there, so if you want to take an online seminar or find a live class, there are sure to be ones in your area. What you need to know to get started is how to set SMART goals: Specific, Measurable, Attainable, Relevant, and Time-based.

SMART GOALS

- SMART goals can help you launch and choose the direction of your business –

Let's give you an example:

S- I want to grow tomatoes to sell to my community
M- I will grow and sell 50 lbs. of tomatoes
A- I'll have to plant 15 plants to achieve 50 lbs. of sellable fruit
R- Tomatoes are a popular product in our area
T- I will hit this goal by the end of summer

You can set goals for how many social media followers you want your business to gather, for how many plants you want to grow in a certain year, to how much you'd like to make in sales. Set some short-, medium-, and long-term goals for yourself and use them to formulate a five-year plan. Customer retention should be one of your main focuses, so think about how you can provide a quality product and superior customer service to achieve this. Take advantage of the free advertising options that today's social media affords you. Who is your target client, and how can you reach them? Is it worth taking out paid advertising in local news outlets and community magazines to reach a demographic that might not be internet or social media savvy? These are decisions that only you can make.

Once you've got a solid client base, how can you keep them engaged and have them spread the word about your business? Giveaways are a great idea, and using social media to enact them works great because you can set the rules. Entries in return for sharing posts are a terrific, free way to get your current clients and followers to pass along your information to their family and friends. Always back up your promises when it comes to giveaways. Being accessible to your clients is another good way to build and retain clientele. Make sure you post available phone hours on your website and social media profiles and have a valid, professional email address where customers can reach you. Check it at least once a day and answer inquiries in a timely fashion.

Remember that a gardening business is a business just like any other and requires that you have a plan, clientele, and good operating practices. Be creative, be practical, and always keep in mind that you can start small and expand later as both your gardening skills and your business sense improve. A market garden can be a lucrative and exciting endeavor, and you will meet a ton of wonderful people and build relationships with other businesses and your customers. Just keep impeccable records, provide good customer service, and focus on the quality of your product, and you'll be good to go.

And that's that! We've reached the end of our time together, and we're so excited that you came on this gardening journey with us. The knowledge you gained here will carry you through the beginning stages of your gardening enterprise, and whether you choose to monetize or not, you'll soon be growing flavorful, healthy food for you and your family in a garden you designed and built with your own hands. There isn't much in the world that can come close to the feeling of picking the first juicy tomato or crisp cucumber that you nurtured from a tiny seed to a full-grown fruit. It's magical. And delicious, which might be even better. Enjoy your garden, and thanks for choosing us to be your guide!

Conclusion

Thank you for reading *Growing Vegetables*. We're grateful that you've given us the opportunity to show you the amazing world of market gardening. This book was a labor of love for us, and we hope you'll revisit these pages often when you need a refresher or want to grow some vegetables you haven't tried yet! We went through a lot of information very quickly, so please don't feel like you have to memorize it all. The best books are the ones you can return to like an old friend when you need advice.

Within these chapters, you learned all the stages of gardening, from site selection to designing, building, planting, and maintenance. We also covered a lot of basic botany and soil science. When you've got a solid grasp on those fundamentals, you can learn to grow just about anything. One of the best things about being a gardener is that you get to be a lifelong student. There is always something new and exciting to learn, and it's a world of fun to go down the research rabbit hole. When you settle into being a gardener, you will find certain aspects you want to specialize in. Some people are obsessed with soil health, some are in the pursuit of the perfect tomato, and others still like to focus on things like companion planting and edible landscaping (look it up, it's really cool!)

The point is that this book was specifically written with beginners in mind, and it's opened a door for you into a vast world of gardening just waiting to be explored. We want you to find a passion and run with it. And if you want to turn your passion into a business, we've given you the basics on how to do that, too. You should, of course, check all your state and local regulations before you start any undertaking, but most areas have pretty straightforward codes governing food-based businesses. Taking the time to make sure you're following those codes will give you legitimacy, cover your assets, and ensure that you won't be subject to scrutiny or, worse, fines and citations.

We want you to be a happy, successful market gardener, but even if you never sell a product, we want you to be satisfied with your personal gardening experience. The knowledge you've gained by reading through this book will be enough to get you and your family growing your own healthy, fresh vegetables. Gardening makes a wonderful family activity, too. Even the littlest helpers can pull weeds and learn how to water, and harvesting is fun for everyone. As a bonus, kids are given an early lesson on where food comes from and are always more inclined to try vegetables that they've had a hand in growing.

The biggest lesson we want you to take away from *Growing Vegetables* is that you are building an ecosystem. When you're vigilant about building a garden in the best location to avoid damage to the landscape, and you treat your soil with care, you've created the footprint of that new ecosystem. By planting and maintaining your garden using all the best practices and make sure to rejuvenate the soil every year with organic material and crop rotation, you'll have a thriving plot you can enjoy for many years. Thanks again for reading, and if you loved the book, please hop on over and give us a nice review- we'd appreciate it. Happy gardening, and we'll see you next time!

Made in the USA
Columbia, SC
01 August 2021